MIND, BODY AND WEALTH

PAVILION SERIES
General Editor: F. G. Bailey

Also in this series:

STRATAGEMS AND SPOILS
A Social Anthropology of Politics
F. G. BAILEY

GIFTS AND POISON
The Politics of Reputation
edited by F. G. BAILEY

DEBATE AND COMPROMISE
The Politics of Innovation
edited by F. G. BAILEY

NEW HEAVEN, NEW EARTH
A Study of Millenarian Activities
KENELM BURRIDGE

THE CHILDREN OF ISRAEL
The Bene Israel of Bombay
SCHIFRA STRIZOWER

FRIENDS OF FRIENDS
Networks, Manipulators and Coalitions
JEREMY BOISSEVAIN

MIND, BODY AND WEALTH

A Study of Belief and Practice
in an Indian Village

D. F. POCOCK

Reader in Social Anthropology
Dean of the School of African and Asian Studies
University of Sussex

PAVILION SERIES

SOCIAL ANTHROPOLOGY

OXFORD
BASIL BLACKWELL

ISBN 0 631 15000 5 Cloth bound edition

Printed in Great Britain by
Western Printing Services Ltd, Bristol
and bound by Kemp Hall Bindery, Oxford

To the memory of Puruṣottam Jhavarbhai Patel

Om. Shri Krishna is my refuge. Having suffered the profound pain and anguish of a thousand long years' separation from Him, I dedicate to the blessed Krishna my body, mind and other faculties, and my wife, house, property and all my wealth together with myself. I am thy slave, O Krishna.

(Formula of dedication for the Vaishnavite at his initiation.)

Contents

Acknowledgements

My thanks are due to All Souls' College, Oxford for the travel grant which aided me in my field-work. I wish also to thank my secretary, Mrs. Douglas Champion for her patience in handling a succession of revisions. Finally, I am grateful to my friends, Michael Howes and Donald Winch for reading the text and suggesting improvements.

Preface

In this book I describe an area of Indian belief, and changes
which appear to be taking place within it. It may seem rather
perverse of me to refer to an area of belief instead of speaking
directly about religion. Nevertheless, I am reluctant to use
this word for two main reasons: in the first place we cannot
dissociate the word from its history; there is no doubt that the
word religion has, in the West, come to connote an area of the
special, a mode of reasoning about the universe governed by
rules which are not those of day-to-day thought. Whether we
think of ourselves as being 'religious' or 'not religious', *the*
religious remains, however much churchmen may lament, a
separate area of life in the West. This separateness tends to
infect anthropological discussion of the topic to such an
extent that religious behaviour, as opposed to any other kind,
political or economic for example, calls for the introduction
of special premises or assumptions about human nature. In
the account which follows I have not felt it necessary to make
any special assumptions nor, even, to use the word religion.
The reader may judge for himself whether his understanding
suffers on that account.

My second objection derives, no doubt, from a reaction
against a great deal of high-flown writing about Hinduism,
by authors who, often, freely admit that we cannot speak of
Hinduism as we speak of Christianity or Islam. However
much such writings feed the romantic interest in the mystical
East, they seem to me to have little to say about the people

who are said to hold these beliefs. One such author, by implication, admits as much. Professor R. C. Zaehner in his book
Hinduism says that 'One of the parodoxes of Hinduism has
always been the yawning gap that separates its higher manifestations from the frankly superstitious and magical practices that go to make up the religious fare of the rural masses.'
(O.U.P., 1962, p. 246.) In what sense is this a paradox? If we
were trying to understand Christianity as a social and historical fact should we limit ourselves solely to the Sermon on the
Mount and dismiss the holy rivalries of Spanish villages?
Should we take St. Paul's condemnation of witchcraft as the
last word on the matter, or should we find out what it is that
European peasants have believed in the past and do believe
now? I hope to show in this book that there is no 'yawning
gap' between beliefs which Professor Zaehner might think
'superstitious' and the rarefied thought of the sectarian philosophies. These are connected not only in the minds of
individual men but interlinked through social relations to
constitute that whole which is inevitably hidden from the
student of texts.

The desire to bring the people to the fore—Professor
Zaehner's 'masses'—leads me to adopt a mode of presentation
which is not that of the conventional ethnographic mono-
graph. But I am urged towards this mode of presentation for
an additional reason. I have written primarily for under-
graduates, in sympathy with their often-voiced sense of the
gulf between the formal analyses in their books and the life
to which these relate. The very consistency, the rounded-off
quality of the major monographs, often rouses a student's
suspicion, irritation or frustration, as he endeavours to take
imaginative grasp of the human reality and relate his own
life to it. I have, therefore, tried to write a book about particular people whom I knew, in a deliberate attempt to lay
the universals of human nature side by side with the par-
ticularities of an alien culture. I feel for the student who,
reading about the Uborme people of the Uttatedyas delta,

learns that they dote on their sisters' sons and give them yams, but gets no hint of how a man can loathe his sister's son or bitterly resent his mother's brother.

This book will have served its purpose if my account enables a student to understand better not only what people believe but also what they do not believe; how one man's faith is another's superstition, and that for every credulity there is also a doubt.

Finally I would stress that this is a book about a particular people, place and time. Had I given in to the temptation to underscore every observation with this caution it would have been very irritating for the reader. He must now guard himself against the assumption that general propositions are presented here about Gujarat or the whole of India.

1

Introductory—Brothers are Rivals

The story that I want to tell is a commonplace one and I have
deliberately let it ramble on occasion in the hope that, by
the simple description of people and events, it will largely tell
itself. I cannot, however, escape the double responsibility
imposed by my involvement with the people concerned and
the selection hidden beneath the very act of description. I
must therefore give the reader an overall view of the book
and my reasons for ordering it as I have.

The bulk of my material is derived from field-work among
the Patidar, a caste of central Gujarat (see map below). I
describe, in this introductory chapter, their internal organization and, more briefly, their relations with other castes. The
discussion of organization leads me to observe that, although
all the members of any caste are in theory equal, in fact they
are very conscious of their standing in each other's eyes.
Among the Patidar this consciousness is revealed most
strongly in the matter of marriage.[1] As members of the same
caste all Patidar can intermarry; as members of particular
lineages and villages some marriage alliances are more prized
than others; some are unthinkable. Even within one lineage,
especially if it is a large one, some families may make, or wish
to make, marriage alliances superior to those of their kinsmen.
In order to do this they have to show the world that they are,
in some ways, superior to these kinsmen. I describe the
pressures operating for and against this desire for distinction:

it is a real problem because a man is inescapably bound to his kinsmen as brothers and equals, and he is no less inescapably bound to seek the best for himself and his family.

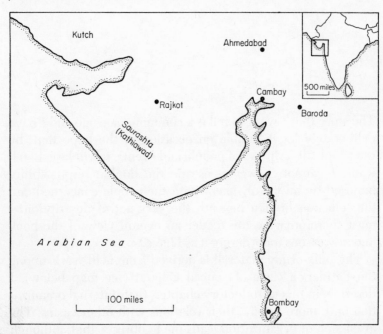

The modern state of Gujarat comprises Kutch and the peninsula of Saurashta; it extends on the mainland from Mt. Abu to the north of Ahmedabad down the western seaboard of the Gulf of Cambay. The Patidar inhabit, for the most part, the area between Ahmedabad and Cambay.

After this introductory chapter I immediately enter into an account of a particular belief, the belief in the evil eye. The transition must seem abrupt: this belief, which I encountered in the early days of field-work, is symptomatic of a whole dimension of village life; it is particularly expressive of the conflict between the desire to do and be well and the fear of appearing superior. Naturally a man desires the good things of life but, if he achieves some of them, must he not fear the envious, evil eye of those who have not been so successful? There is no resolution of this dilemma short of the renunciation of all desire. The discussion of the evil eye concludes with a look at the belief in ghosts which, amongst other things, underscores the earth-bound quality of human wants and the dangers arising from their frustration.

In my third chapter I return to the problem of a group of families which is in the process of seeking distinction within a larger lineage. In doing this I discuss beliefs and actions about *mātā* which are the most prominent spirit beings of the village pantheon but not the most powerful. I describe how beliefs and rituals vary with the social aspirations of the villagers.

The account of *mātā* worship brings out facts which are initially strange to the western mind: the villagers believe that some spiritual beings are impure, for all that they are worshipped and closely related to the daily contingencies of village life. This leads me to show how a pantheon composed of pure and impure gods accords with a world in which pure and impure castes have a symbolic interdependence not only for necessary services but also for mutual definition. A caste defines its relative purity by the relative impurity of another. Once again, if in a different key, we encounter the theme of differentiation and superiority within a common humanity.

Very briefly and figuratively, chapter four can be described as the story of conflict between Shiva and Vishnu. The former, in association with the *mātā*, is seen as ruler of the world of hierarchy based on purity and impurity. The latter becomes, in this part of India, the leader pointing to a different kind of world. In this chapter I reconstruct, as best I can, the older cult of Shiva so that the reader can the better appreciate changes in belief and affiliation directed towards Vishnu.

Vaishnavism, the worship of Vishnu, is associated with the doctrine of divine love which is in essence egalitarian. It is expressed in the veneration of holy men, in hymns and, pre-eminently, in the sect. I discuss all these things in chapter five and, through the discussion of one powerful Vaishnavite sect, I try to show the way in which sects come into being.

The emergence of sects points to a profound paradox in this complex world. The holy man is one who has broken away from the world of desire and possessions, of status and discrimination, purity and impurity; the sect, which is inspired by his teaching, is fully involved in this very world that he has renounced.[2]

In chapter five I discuss this relation of sect to the world of caste. Here I give an account of a modern and influential Gujarati sect. I suggest that, more than any other, its teaching moves towards a break with the world of symbiosis. It accommodates the values of caste but tends to subordinate them to its authority.

In a brief concluding chapter I refer to a schismatic movement within this sect which has been able to carry the ascendancy over caste a step further. It has succeeded to such a degree that it now wins the adherence of the modern city dweller and the emigrant. The message of the holy man, unalloyed by the influence of caste, seems peculiarly fitted to those who have also, in their way, left the world of caste behind them.

A typical Indian village is inhabited by representatives of different castes: of these castes one, usually the largest, is referred to by social anthropologists as the dominant caste. It is called dominant not because it is necessarily the largest but because it owns the largest amount of land in the village and tends, therefore, to have a preponderant say in its politics. A caste which is dominant in one village is usually dominant in many neighbouring villages, and in this way we can refer to one caste as being the dominant caste of the whole area. Within a village the castes are thought of as living in separate areas. I say 'thought of' because this does not always correspond to the reality. A caste may have its local centre in the village but it is not rigidly confined to that area. Pressure on land and a variety of other circumstances oblige single families to live where there is space to build or where there is a house vacant. The only caste which one may expect to find firmly limited to its traditional area is the untouchable caste of the village and of the area.

The Patidar of Central Gujarat are in many respects a typical dominant caste and the villages in which they live correspond to the general pattern outlined. In their villages, however, the idea that castes inhabit separate areas is probably less in force than in villages elsewhere in India. This, I believe, is a result of the history of the Patidar and it will be necessary to say a little about how they have become the dominant caste in this part of Gujarat.

In the early nineteenth century, shortly after the British had moved into Gujarat, they reported the existence of an industrious agricultural caste called the Kanbi. Among these Kanbi some families were known as Patidar because they had a particular right granted to them by the Mogul government which enabled them to dispense with middle-men when paying their land tax. These Patidar families were, for the most part, centred in the Kaira District of Gujarat which is is also a very fertile tract of land. As a result of this fertility and of their privileges the Patidar very rapidly rose, in the course of the nineteenth century, to a position of relative affluence in the local society, and the very name Patidar came to have considerable prestige. Many Kanbi families, who had not in fact enjoyed this particular privilege, came to call themselves Patidar and thus associated themselves with their wealthier and more prestigious caste fellows. This is a process which is very common in India and we have many instances of titles which have become common names. There are, of course, analogous situations in our own society. As the name Patidar became more and more general in the caste so the old name Kanbi fell increasingly into disrepute. By the time of the 1931 census the word Patidar was so commonly used in this caste, and the name Kanbi had become so opprobrious that it was officially discontinued and the caste came to be known as Patidar. The Patidar were, and still are, recognised as holding the highest status under the Brahmans in the local hierarchy of this part of Gujarat.

I have compressed into a few lines a development which took place over a hundred years and inevitably this makes for simplification. When one speaks of a caste as being dominant one very often gives the impression that it is, so to speak, uniformly dominant throughout the area. One tends to give the impression that each of its members is as wealthy and as prestigious as the others. This is a very misleading impression. As the overall condition of the caste improved, the original Patidar families of the early nineteenth century maintained, for the greater part, their position in relation to other families. When we survey the Patidar caste today, therefore, we find that, although as a caste it occupies a very high place in the local hierarchy, it has within it considerable variation in economic and social conditions. There are Patidar families who live in large, almost palatial, houses, and who, by any standards, enjoy a high standard of living. At the other end of the scale there are Patidar whose sole territorial possession is the mud hut in which they live, who work as labourers in the fields of other Patidar, and whose standard of living does not rise above the subsistence level. Such people can only be said to enjoy status in the eyes of other castes by association with their wealthier caste fellows. Although such people enjoy a certain prestige, it would be absurd to say that they were as effectively dominant as a wealthy caste fellow who owned enough land to grow substantial cash crops like tobacco and cotton as well as his own food crops. Such a wealthy Patidar might also have direct interest in a business in Bombay or Ahmedabad or an indirect interest through a kinsman. In general he would have patronage and power as well as a variety of interests to preserve and expand. Even a Patidar in what we might call the middle range of the caste, who had a sufficiency of land to produce his own food, and perhaps a small amount of cash crops, would not necessarily find himself in a position of unchallenged political and economic superiority over a member of another caste. To take the most common and effective form of patronage that we find at the village level as an index of a man's potential power over others, such a man in the middle range would probably neither need nor be in a position to hire the labour of others.

I believe that it is because the Patidar have risen from low to high status in a relatively short period of time, and also because this rise in status has not been reflected by a uniform advance in economic conditions throughout the caste that the Patidar do not, by and large, maintain those master–servant relationships with other castes known elsewhere in India as *jajmāni* relationships. If other accounts are to be believed, although I suspect that an element of romanticism has crept into some of them, the castes of areas and therefore of villages are inter-linked by traditional service relationships of various kinds. The families of the dominant caste are represented as lords of the manor, who, in return for the protection and food they provide for their dependants, receive a variety of services from the priest, from the potter, barber, carpenter and so on. Traditionally these relationships are relationships between families and are inherited so that the son of a carpenter has a right to serve the son of his father's master. The value of such a right is considerable in a country where under-employment is chronic. To have a patron meant, traditionally, not only that one would not starve, but also that one could expect political protection, interest-free loans and other benefits. There is some evidence that a few of the wealthy original Patidar families settled families of these specialized castes in their villages with, presumably, the intention of establishing the kind of traditional system which I have outlined. Thus in the past power was converted into status as the wealthy landlord created his own caste hierarchy beneath him. But among the descendants of such families today there is very little evidence of it; among the majority of Patidar there is no tradition of such relationships and little evidence of interest in them. A Patidar who can afford it will employ the barber in his village or the washerman or, if he has need, a carpenter, but I have rarely found any belief that such relationships are tied or hereditary or, indeed, that they entail rights and duties going beyond the particular service contracted for at a particular moment. A man may well use the local washerman for the most part, but when he wishes to have his clothes cleaned for some special occasion he can take them to the local town without incurring guilt or the criticism of his neighbours. In general, among the Patidar, I found that the word *jajmān* was either not known or completely misunderstood.

Other dominant castes in India must have, according to their size, the same range of economic variation within them as the Patidar. I do not think that the relative disinterest which the Patidar display in maintaining traditional patterns of dependence is to be related directly to the fact that a large part, if not the majority, of the caste is incapable of maintaining such relationships on a large scale, although, no doubt, this is a supporting factor. I would attribute their indifference rather to the relative speed with which they have risen in the local hierarchy and the period in which that rise took place, a period which saw the introduction and the spread of Western secular values and materialism.

The Patidar are also indifferent to another appurtenance of high status—the famous sacred thread of the Hindu. According to the sacred literature this is one of the marks of the twice-born and therefore something to be acquired by members of a caste having pretensions of high status in traditional Indian society. We have evidence from other places in India, and from other times, that castes whose members were not in the habit of wearing this thread persuaded Brahmans to invest them with it once they began to change their ideas about their place in the traditional society, in other words, as they began to rise in the local hierarchy. The Patidar, however, appear for the greater part to have been totally indifferent to an external sign which, throughout India and for centuries, has been regarded as the distinctive external sign of the high caste man. Even quite poor and uneducated Patidar felt free to describe the custom to me as the Gujarat equivalent of 'a load of old rubbish'. In this connexion I might add another feature which makes the Patidar somewhat atypical among dominant castes in India. In those areas where the traditional *jajmāni* relationships are reported it is usual to find that one particular caste tends to call upon the services of one particular Brahman caste for the performance of its family rituals, notably marriage. The higher a caste is in the local hierarchy, the more it will tend towards this kind of exclusiveness. Among the Patidar I find no such relation. There are many Brahman castes in Gujarat and some are congregated more in some areas than in others, and for this reason the Patidar of those areas are more likely to call upon them than upon others. But I never heard that it was a mark of superior status to be served by this Brahman rather than that and, indeed, in one and the same village, if more than one Brahman caste was represented there, the different Patidar families would call upon the services of either with indifference.

This all relates back, I believe, to the relative lack of caste segregation in the village. When I compare the Patidar with more orthodox, or traditionally minded, castes in Western Gujarat and in Kutch, I would say that they are considerably less concerned with their status *vis-à-vis* other castes; on the other hand each head of a Patidar family is more concerned with his standing *vis-à-vis* other Patidar.

This brings us to the internal organization of the caste. I have already said that there is considerable variety of economic and social conditions among the Patidar. This variety tends to be reflected in each village in which the Patidar live but, nevertheless, one can say that the economic condition of one village or a cluster of villages is relatively uniform in relation to another village or cluster of villages.

In this way we can refer to an economic hierarchy within the caste such that there is, at the top, a group of wealthy and prestigious villages and at the bottom a larger number of poor villages. The poorer Patidar can lay claim to high status only by nominal association with their caste fellows and have none of the resources or appurtenances which their wealthier caste fellows enjoy.

This economic hierarchy is recognized by the Patidar and reflected in the pattern of their marriages. There is a widespread belief among the rural population, supported by the ancient Sanskrit legal literature, that the family of the bride is inferior to the family of the groom. The emphasis upon this belief, and the extent to which it is reflected in the organization of their social life, vary from caste to caste. In some castes it is what we should call a 'token' belief, limited to a ritual expression and having no further implication for the two families concerned. But among the Patidar the belief is strong and supports the economic hierarchy. The quality of the marriages which a man is able to contract on behalf of his daughters reflects very considerably upon his own standing. From the earliest reports in the nineteenth century up to the present time it is clear that the desire to marry his daughter well amounts to an obsession for the average Patidar father. Still today a man will count his life well spent if he has married his daughters into families having a superior standing to his own, even if he has bankrupted himself in the process. The greater the disparity between the standing of the bride's family and that of the groom, the greater will be the dowry which the girl's father must pay; although few can afford enormous dowries bridging over great differences in social standing, each man strives to contract for his daughter a marriage alliance with a family somewhat superior to his own. There is, therefore, an inevitability of expense.

Given the economic difference between and within villages, it follows that marriage into certain villages carries more prestige than marriage into others. But, and the Patidar themselves recognize this, the word village here is used as a convenient shorthand to refer to a cluster of lineages which go to make up the Patidar population of that village. This becomes clear enough when I say that not every single Patidar family in a village necessarily participates in the overall reputation of that village. In very poor villages there may be relatively well-to-do men who are in a position to accumulate sufficient money to contract marriages far outside the range of their fellow villagers. Similarly even in the most aristocratic villages there are slum areas inhabited by families and whole lineages of impoverished Patidar. No one would seek out a marriage alliance with such families simply because they happened to live in that particular village.

The reference to lineages suggests that the Patidar attach great significance to the value of descent, and this is true. It may seem paradoxical therefore when I say that the impoverished lineages, or families, may well be as legitimately descended from the founder of the village as the highest ranking lineage within it. It is by no means unusual to find that even the senior, most ancient, lineage in the village is at the same time the poorest and the least respected. The apparent paradox arises from a failure on our part to understand the Patidar problem which emerges from a conflict in their values. They do indeed attach great importance to what, in our society, we call 'social mobility'. We may put the matter briefly by saying that a Patidar prides himself as a social person on two counts which may be contradictory: on the one hand he looks to the past, to his father and to his father's fathers; on the other hand he looks to the future and to the superior status which his grandchildren will have by virtue of the marriage which he has contracted for their mother. There is considerable evidence to indicate that the circumstances of modern life favour the latter value and that, although the Patidar continue to speak of lineages, the generation depth of lineages has shrunk in the course of this century as their number has increased. In the past we might find the Patidar of one village distributed among, say, three lineages each one named after a distant ancestor. Today, with increasing rapidity, small sections of three or four generations' depth, and even individual families, establish separate social identities for themselves in order to contract superior marriages. Briefly, it is only a slight exaggeration to say that any Patidar who is in a position to do so acts as though he would be the founder of a new lineage; his hopes are frustrated by the fact that his own sons share, individually, the same ambition.

The genealogy between pages 16 and 17 records the descent and marriage details of the largest lineage in the village of Sundarana in the Kaira District of Gujarat. It illustrates, economically, much of what I have been saying, and at the same time it introduces the village from which the bulk of the material in this book is drawn. The lineage is known collectively as the Prabhu Lakhujivalla after the founding father Prabhu, the son of Lakhu. The bulk of its population inhabits one sector of the village, but there are some families quite separated from it, in particular the descendants of Vallabh to whom I shall return in a moment. As is clear from the chart, Prabhu Lakhuji had five sons of whom Kālidās was the eldest and Vallabh the youngest. From the sons of Prabhu Lakhuji is descended a population, with their wives and children, of well over three hundred, but in the eyes of their fellow villagers there are only two sections which are significant. On the one hand they see the descendants of Kālidās, Kuvar, Mitha and Kāshiyā and on the other are the descendants of Vallabh.

Even to the outside observer the grounds of this distinction are obvious. The area in which the former group lives is a squalid and congested one, the dwellings are for the most part small wattle and daub huts and the pathways which connect them are narrow, and thick with mud. A family of five people, that I know well, lives in a narrow room six yards by three, the grandfather's half of a division between two brothers made thirty years ago. The Prabhu Lakhuji section is to the south-east of Sundarana, one of the oldest inhabited areas of the village. The descendants of Vallabh live, for the most part, in the recently developed south-west section. The very phrase 'recently developed' gives immediately an index of their social condition: the typical situation is for a growing population to confine itself in the same area by division and sub-division of property. The fact that an area can be said to be recently developed implies that its owners have a super-fluity of land on which they can afford to build, not to mention the financial resources to cover the cost of materials and buildings. The descendants of Vallabh live in small but solid brick houses with small courtyards and sufficient stabling room for at least two buffalo. They cultivate their own lands, but are in a position to hire extra labour at sowing time and at harvest; their best clothes are not the same as their working clothes; their children are healthy and their young men do not yet show the signs of incipient muscle wastage which prematurely ages their cousins in the older quarter. The difference between these two sections is rather marked and perhaps more so than is commonly the case. For this very reason it provides a good example of the kind of thing which is happening all the time in Patidar villages.

It would be quite impossible to give the individual history of each family which has contributed to the present state of affairs, and obviously there are those incalculable factors which we lump together under the heading of luck. Never-theless there are certain basic facts which will, other circum-stances favouring, set a family on the road to good fortune, and others which, without favouring circumstances, forbode almost certain hardship. For example, if a man has many daughters and few or no sons, it means that he is obliged to spend on the dowries of his daughters and has no hope of recouping his financial position through dowries which sons receive. On the other hand, of course, a man who has several sons and few or no daughters is in a very advantageous position. When there is only one son in the family and when this situation is repeated regularly in the course of a few generations, the family is normally in rather prosperous circumstances. In other families, where there is more than one son, the property will almost certainly be divided, and it must be divided equally between the sons not long after the father's death. A family which is not subject to such division not merely preserves its property entire, but is more likely to be in a position to increase it.

Here we have another of the inevitable contradictions of peasant life in India. The more sons a man has the prouder he is and, among the Patidar, the more his financial position is likely to be very satisfactory as a result. At the same time, the more sons there are the greater is the risk of fragmentation of the family land into small, scarcely viable, plots of ground. Those who have some wealth can, of course, invest it, and the education of his children is probably one of the most common investments for the Indian villager. The particular good fortune of the descendants of Vallabh has been that they owned land on that side of the village nearest to the wealthy Dharmaj where some Patidar families had established an irrigation business and were interested in establishing one of their pumps on Sundarana land. Some of the descendants of Vallabh came in with the Dharmaj Patidar as partners in an irrigation works and others of them found regular employment in the works. This new situation provided immediate and obvious economic benefits in a society in which few are assured of a regular weekly wage but it also provided the intangible and more traditional benefits of wealthy patronage by the Dharmaj partners. The descendants of Vallabh were now in a position to put in a good word for their kinsmen, not only for employment in the local irrigation works, but also in a large range of small-scale industries owned in Dharmaj.

What has still to be understood, however, is how and why the descendants of Vallabh are separating themselves from the larger body. It is easier to answer the second question first. The reason why the descendants of Vallabh wish to be dissociated from all the other descendants of Prabhu Lakhuji is that they want to have a separate identity in marriage negotiations. If they continue to be included within the larger group, then any inferior marriage or low behaviour reflects upon all the members of that group: that such 'inferior' customs as widow-remarriage and the employment of the family's womenfolk in field labour are only the product of poverty is not weighed in the account. The descendants of Vallabh can scarcely hope to get their daughters married well, with relatively low dowries, and also to receive substantial dowries from their daughters-in-law, so long as they are associated in the public mind with such a large group of relatively inferior Patidar.

There is nothing formal or sudden about the process of segmentation. Each of the groups descended from one of the sons of Prabhu Lakhuji has, so to speak, its own identity, and the members of each such group have some sense of kinship closer than that which they share with the entire lineage. The solidarity of such groupings in no way threatens the identity of the entire lineage any more than the solidarity of one particular family within it might be said to do so. Some anthropologists, adopting a kind of shorthand, sometimes give the impression that a clan, a tribe or a lineage splits up in some mysterious ways analogous to the splitting off of cells in a biological process. Even those who appreciate the role of the individual in such social processes all too often tend to impute motivation to him, and suggest that all his actions, seen with the wisdom of hindsight, are directed towards the end finally achieved—the setting up of a relatively autonomous group. For people who have first-hand experience of such situations the whole account is imbued with a sense of unreality. For this reason I describe, as best I can, the history of the growth of heightened identity among the descendants of Vallabh.

The very fact that the descendants of Vallabh live apart

from the traditional area of the lineage indicates some earlier inferiority. Had they been people of substance they would in the past have owned sufficient territory in the traditional area to maintain themselves there. The fact that today they occupy a recently inhabited area suggests that they were earlier driven out as a result of political or economic pressure, conceivably both. But for favouring circumstances, notably their proximity to the wealthy developers of Dharmaj, there is no reason to suppose that they would be in a position to establish themselves as a separate group today. It is not even the case that all the different families who are descended from Vallabh have independent resources of their own. In fact there seem to be only two men of substance in the group who have diffused their prestige and to a certain extent their economic benefits throughout the whole. These two are Kishor (1) and Hāthi (2).[3] The latter is an only son whose father invested rather more than was usual at the time in his education. He is the only man in the village who possesses a radio and regularly receives a daily newspaper. He is a source of information about the world at large, and very much a counsellor for most people in the village when they have dealings with the local bureaucracy or government. The former owned less land originally. If we assume, as is indeed likely, that the property has been equally divided from generation to generation according to traditional Hindu law, we can see from the genealogy that Kishor has inherited only a third as much land as Hāthi and, indeed, is lucky in that he had no brother with whom he would have had to divide his inheritance. Kishor left the village when he was a young man and worked in Bombay, where he acquired some basic knowledge of machinery, and only returned in his late twenties. His great good fortune is that it was his land which was chosen for the establishment of the irrigation works. I might add that he had to fight for the right to dispose of his land to the Dharmaj Patidar as his fellow villagers resented this intrusion of outsiders. By a mixture of force and dip-

lomacy, by, for example, providing free clean water to the villagers, Kishor established himself as the manager of the irrigation works in partnership with the Dharmaj Patidar. He is now in a position not only to give jobs in the irrigation works, but, through the receipt of a regular salary, to increase his property at the expense of less well-to-do fellow villagers. Kishor has, in addition, five sons and no daughters and has every prospect of receiving fairly substantial dowries with his daughters-in-law whose fathers would be happy to be associated with so well placed a man.

It would be misleading to suppose that either Kishor or Hāthi, or both of them, at any point has sat down and considered the strategy of secession. It is rather the case that secession is forced upon them, not only by the expectation of their own kinsmen but also by the expectation which all the villagers have of the behaviour appropriate to a relatively wealthy man.

It so happens that Kishor is married to a rather mean woman who does not enjoy keeping the kind of open house which several other women in the village do. Nevertheless she is obliged by virtue of her husband's standing in the village to maintain a certain standard and cannot, at least publicly, indulge in some of the economies which she would prefer. In addition to maintaining a generally higher standard of living in day-to-day affairs she is obliged to observe various ritual occasions from which, if her husband were not earning so well, she might well be excused. This means that she must prepare and distribute certain sweets on special occasions, holy days and the like, and on any special occasion which normally might be celebrated by the family alone she must invite at least one representative from each of the houses occupied by the descendants of Vallabh.

There is a convention—one cannot call it more than that—among the villagers that the group constituted by the descendants of a great-grandfather is a convenient one for celebrations and sharing. If a man is celebrating a particularly

C

good tobacco harvest, shall we say, he can invite the members of this group without causing any offence to other people in the village. This and similar occasions are contrasted very much with the big and formal occasions of marriage and death. On such occasions a man is expected to invite a much wider group, and his failure either to invite, or to attend, on such an occasion is evidence on his part that he no longer wishes to be associated with the wider group. Such action has not been taken by the descendants of Vallabh in relation to their wider lineage, and I doubt whether any such action would be taken deliberately. One would expect rather that just as a man feels no great obligation to invite a kinsman connected by five generations to a domestic celebration so, as the generations which separate the descendants of Vallabh from the descendants of Prabhu Lakhuji increase, the relationship will gradually wither away.

It would be considered very arrogant, rude and not at all befitting a man of status to spurn his poorer relatives in this way. Nevertheless, I was told of several occasions in other villages where, as one particular family or section of a lineage increased in wealth and thereby in the lavishness of its entertainment and the like, so other relatives became more and more ashamed about receiving hospitality which they could in no way return. There is a rather pleasing irony in the situation in that the wealthier relative by apparent hospitality and generosity can be said, almost literally, to choke off his poorer relatives with whom he would prefer not to be associated. The action of separation and therefore the blame, if there is any, falls upon the poorer relative and not upon the wealthy man. But this is to take a cynical and an outsider's view of the matter. Given the values of Patidar society a good man who is in a position to do so, simply by being hospitable and helpful, emerges to a position of eminence in his society with which poorer relatives cannot compete. Kishor and Hāthi are men of substance for the entire population of the village regardless of caste, and it is inevitable therefore that the four generations from Vallabh's grandson Jora should, from the villagers' point of view, naturally participate in their substance.

What, however, of the families descended from Ragnāth (4) and Bechar (5) who are accepted as descendants of Vallabh, but whose exact connexion is not known either by themselves or by the group with which we have been dealing? Both groups exemplify the apparently astonishing indifference of some Patidar to genealogical details once these cease to have social significance for them. We can certainly say that the fact that neither group recalls, with any certainty, its connexion with Vallabh, is an indication that the prosperity of the descendants of the latter is a relatively recent occurrence. We may be sure that if the descendants of Vallabh do come to be known as a completely separate group within the village these, at present, dissociated lineages will establish the exact connexion.

In order to understand their association among the descendants of Vallabh we might look at the more general reaction of the descendants of Prabhu Lakhuji to their wealthier kinsmen. First of all, they not only like to count among their number such distinguished kinsmen as Kishor and Hāthi, it is also advantageous to them when negotiating marriages with families in other villages to be able to point to such kinsmen. In some villages the very number of brick houses, as opposed to mud huts, is a matter of pride to people, even though they have never been invited into such houses, nor stand any chance of ever being invited. From this point of view the descendants of Prabhu Lakhuji must wish all success to the descendants of Vallabh, to the extent that they hope to participate in their honour. But they recognize that if the descendants of Vallabh really do establish themselves as a separate social identity in the eyes of other villages, then this can only be done at the expense of their association with Prabhu Lakhuji. On these grounds and for more immediately practical reasons they have no desire to offend Kishor, Hāthi and their kinfolk. The descendants of Vallabh, for their part, are not yet sufficiently large in number nor really so influential that they can afford to flout the relationship with the wider lineage, even should they wish to do so, which is improbable. Nevertheless to appear well in their own eyes, in the eyes of their kinsmen and, perhaps more important of all, in the eyes of their affines and potential affines, they must to a certain extent distinguish themselves in the literal sense of the word. In setting themselves up they have need of the increased numbers which the two separated lineages add to their group and also the lineal value which the name Vallabh has by virtue of its relative antiquity. A group of this size and generation depth is in no way remarkable, its members would not normally be referred to as *kulin*, people of lineage and blood. Such a claim could only rest upon a genealogy of at least six generations and preferably more. There is nobody, as I recall, of any particular distinction in these 'separated' lineages although we may note that Somā (6) has six very well married sons, only one daughter and is presumably a man of some substance. The advantages to these lineages of the association under the name of Vallabh are obvious, and need not be repeated.

One whole aspect of this nascent secession cannot be dealt with here, and is not over-obvious from the genealogy. The village of Sundarana belongs to a group of seven villages which, over the generations, have increasingly come to intermarry more amongst themselves than with other villages. Recently this informal association has been formalized. Now members who marry either sons or daughters outside the circle of the seven incur quite substantial fines. The names of the seven villages in addition to Sundarana are Ardi, Bhārel, Jor, Morad, Vānskilyā and Vatāv.

An analysis of the genealogy would show that these names occur with increasing frequency as we approach the present generation. But even the most casual inspection shows that, in many families, marriages have recently been contracted outside the circle of these seven. In fact, marriage inside the circle is still largely a matter of ideal to be achieved, and to a certain extent a matter of prestige—not something that everybody can afford. And, among those who do marry among the seven, some marry well and some not so well. To take the genealogy in front of us as an example, a man from another village in the seven who married his daughter into the lineage of Vallabh would consider himself, and be considered, to have affines superior to somebody who had married his daughter into a less prestigious lineage of the same village. But a man who had *received* a daughter from the lineage of Vallabh, who had, so to speak, 'scored' according to the rules of hypergamy over an already prestigious lineage, would be considered yet more superior. As a result of this marriage alliance he, if he had daughters, would be in a position to marry them off to good families with a dowry somewhat less than he would have expected to pay had he not contracted such an alliance. What does not emerge from the genealogy is the *quality* of the marriages which the descendants of Vallabh have contracted. It must be accepted here that the lineages in the other villages to which they have allied themselves have status in those villages somewhat similar to their own. Another fact which is not apparent is that where they have married their women into villages outside the circle these outside villages tend to have an overall superior status to the villages of the circle of seven. Although such marriages have been followed by the payment of a fine, the alliances still reflect some honour on the men who contracted them. It is even true to say that the very capacity to pay the fine and not be financially embarrassed by it gives credit to a man. His fellows adopt an ambiguous attitude towards him somewhat similar to that adopted by the other descendants of Prabhu Lakhuji to the potential secession of Vallabh's group. They disapprove of the separatist action and at the same time enjoy, and benefit by, the reflected glory. A good affinal relationship established by any member of the village, wherever the affines may be located, establishes for his fellow villagers the *possibility* of following up that alliance by another, *possibly* at somewhat reduced expense. However, it seems that, for the present, the idea that the good marriage should take place within the circle of the seven holds as an ideal for all the members of the village, even though there are some who have not been able to achieve it or to achieve it in its entirety. Those fathers in inferior lineages who hope to marry a daughter or a son among the seven will look to their kinsmen among the descendants of Vallabh to put in a good word for them among their own affines; since the affines of the descendants of Vallabh are influential men in their own villages they can do much to make or to prevent a marriage contract.

The Patidar peasantry are much concerned with self-improvement and so with change. The Patidar of Sundarana do not, admittedly, conceive of an entirely new structure of human relationships, but they are very ready to embrace the idea of constant reorganization of the relationships within that structure. They are fully conscious also, that in order to improve his condition a man, a family, or an entire caste, must abandon certain customs and take on certain others. In this sense they can be said to live historically. Over against the traditional image of the Indian peasant locked in the cage of unchanging ordinances, they freely use the very common word *sudhāravuṅ*—a term which can best be translated 'to better oneself' or 'to improve'. But improvement is always at someone else's expense. This effect flows from the principle of hierarchy which governs all classification in traditional India.

A comparison with our own way of thinking should make this clear. Our societies in the West are governed by the ideal of equality. Particularly when we talk about international economics, there is sometimes an underlying assumption that all the societies of the world are working towards some kind of balance, a state of fair shares for all. In order to preserve this fantasy, to the extent that we think about it all, we assume either that development of technology in the West will slow down or stop, or that its progressive achievements will, in some miraculous way, be instantaneously diffused to the ends of the earth and the fruits simultaneously enjoyed by the entire population of the world. Many of our plans and policies are ostensibly devised in the light of this quite unrealistic vision. The reader has only to consider how impossible, and even repulsive, he would find any alternative, to realize that we are at a stage in the history of our thought at which we cannot even entertain the idea of institutionalized and permanent inequality. This, as Louis Dumont has emphasized, is the fundamental difference between India and the West.

For the Patidar the idea of the good life implies immediately superiority, superiority over someone else. Moreover, when a man has achieved a position of relative affluence, he does not suppose that those whom he has left behind now unite in offering him generous congratulations, and acquiesce in the inferiority for themselves which his elevation implies. Here another classical image, of the lowly Indian peasant humbly accepting that station in life to which his *karma* has brought him, must be abandoned. The ambivalent attitude of kinsmen towards those who are in the process of secession, or who have seceded, sufficiently indicates that the real situation is more complex than it is commonly presented.

At the lower levels of the caste hierarchy, below the Patidar, that is to say, one finds the same ambivalence of attitude expressed more extremely. Among the Untouchables, for example, there is a real hatred of the Patidar, shot through with envy. Unable as yet to conceive an entirely different order of things they must admire those who have what they lack, and this turns hatred into a resentful acquiescence. If the doctrine of *karma* explains human misfortune it provides no comfort. There are, however, other doctrines which speak of individuality and of equality. Over against the belief in an anonymous soul passing from birth to birth, there is set the conception of the individualized soul capable of choosing and clinging to a divine lord: thus liberation from the cycle of rebirth, *moksha*, is achieved.

NOTES

1. For a more detailed account of the Patidar and the significance of marriage, see my *Kanbi and Patidar*, Clarendon Press, 1972.
2. For the authoritative statement on this, see L. Dumont, 'World Renunciation in Indian Religions', *Contributions to Indian Sociology*, ed. Dumont and Pocock, No. VIII (Mouton, 1965); reprinted in Louis Dumont, *Religion/Politics, and History in India*, Mouton, 1970.
3. Numbers in brackets relate to the genealogy between pp. 16 and 17.

2

The Evil Eye—Envy and Greed

Momad[1] put on my raincoat and a large 1930s style trilby hat, known as a double-crowned Terai, and, looking to my eyes rather sinister, pranced up the lane to the village. Ten minutes later he was back, crestfallen and carrying the coat over his arm. 'What happened?' I asked. 'Oh it's Surajben' he said, 'she told me to take it off.' 'But why?' I asked. 'Well,' he said, 'people would think I looked too beautiful.' I had scarcely been in the village a month at this time. Why on earth Momad should be thought beautiful in a hat and coat several sizes too large, and badly travel-stained, I could not imagine. 'But why, Momad?' I persisted 'Why shouldn't you look beautiful?' 'People,' he said, 'people would think that these are fine things.' 'But so what if they do?' 'Well,' he replied, 'some people believe I would fall ill—it is *najar*.'

The word *najar*, which in this context I translate as the evil eye, is also in common use with less dramatic meanings such as a 'look', as in 'have a look', or 'sight', as in 'short-sighted'. Before I discuss its malevolent significance any further let me give a more detailed example. This concerns the same Surajben, the wife of Momad's patron in the village, Kishor, and whom Momad, although a Muslim, addressed affectionately as *māsi*—mother's sister.

Some months after the incident of the raincoat Surajben gave birth to her fifth son, Bhailal. Very soon afterwards the baby came out in a rash, which made it fretful and wretched.

Surajben took him to the dispensary in Petlad and followed the doctor's instructions about bathing, powdering and the like. Momad and I went for a walk the evening after she returned from Petlad. 'You remember we were talking about *najar*?' he said. 'Yes, of course.' 'Well, Surajben thinks that Bhailal has been struck by it.' 'Oh really—what's she going to do about it?' I asked. 'She's done it already,' said Momad. He told me that Surajben had put some chillies and a scrap of the child's hair into a small brass bowl. On to these she had put a hot coal and inverted the bowl on a flat metal eating dish. Over this she had poured liquid buffalo dung. The bowl could not then be lifted and this had proved to her that the child was suffering from *najar*. Apparently a less elaborate test would have been to wave chillies round the child's head and throw them in the fire. If the gas from the chillies had escaped there would have been no *najar*, and another cause for the sickness would have had to be found. 'So the baby is suffering from *najar*?' I said, 'what does she do now?' 'We shall have to wait and see,' said Momad.

Within two days things were a little clearer. Surajben's husband's second cousin, Chiman (7), had no children. It seems that he had visited Surajben shortly after the child was born and made some comment about the way it could already move its eyes and notice things. Surajben had decided that this was the source of *najar*. You do not accuse people to their faces in such matters and, indeed, it is usually assumed that the guilty party is unaware of the damage done. Surajben therefore embarked on the following course of treatment: she made a point of visiting more frequently with her husband's kinsman and of inviting him to her house as well. As often as possible she would give him the child to hold; he, frankly fond of children, was always happy to hold it. Surajben was very pleased with the results. She had put a black thread round the baby's neck, as most mothers do by way of added precaution, but by giving the child a daily dose, so to speak, of Chiman's *najar*, its power diminished.

The baby was allegedly always very ill after each treatment, but progressively less and less so, until finally the rash disappeared entirely.

When I saw Bhailal three years later, he was a very healthy and remarkably well-built little boy. Like all mothers who fear the envy of others, Surajben had deprived him of the formal appearances of care. Apart from the black thread with its little brass amulet he wore nothing, and his bleached brown hair grew to his shoulders. Surajben said that he was five years old, and therefore it was five years since I had visited them. I did not argue; Bailhal certainly looked a healthy five-year-old.

Najar, the evil eye, is the eye of envy, and it is an inevitable feature of a world in which men set store by looks, or health, or goods, or any pleasant thing. Even if, as is likely, one sets no store by one's mere subsistence, the very deprivations of others give grounds for fear. Since there is no one who cannot find someone whose plight is in some way worse than his own, so there is no one who is completely immune to envy and so to *najar*. Let me describe some typical *najar* situations. Doors should always be closed while eating otherwise hungry men may look in. Thus if one is eating out of doors, for example in the fields, and someone passes, one should offer him food. If food is offered, and can be accepted on caste grounds, some, be it only a little, should be eaten to demonstrate good will. A man in the village once suffered a fever because when he was drinking tea outside his house a stranger to whom he offered some, had refused it. The fever was only cured after he had given a coconut to the goddess. The stranger in this case was presumed to be deliberately malevolent—*melo manas* (literally—a dirty man). A woman was once feeding her child and looked at it with great affection. Her mother-in-law, fearing for the child, suddenly directed the young woman's attention to the stone flour-mill, which immediately broke in half. Here there is no question of envy, but of permanent evil eye unconsciously exercised.

Envy enters only when we realize that it was the mother-in-law who spread the story through the village![2] A man bought a new hookah of the portable kind and was walking back from the town with it. A passer-by asked him where he had bought it, and it broke at once. A woman had a child and another asked to see it. It died. Whenever you feel that someone is looking at you, immediately pretend to take great interest in some worthless object, and so direct his attention towards that.

Although *najar* can run freely wherever there are human values, it is to a certain extent limited by a kind of realism. My battered hat and stained raincoat together with other marvels such as my typewriter, were not dangerous to me, as far as I could understand, any more than a landlord who lived in a village nearby had anything to fear from his silk shirts. *Najar* seems to be apprehended more from those with whom one is, in most other respects, equal, or has reason to expect to be. In a society governed by hierarchical principles in which status is given by birth, some seem to be naturally in a more favoured position than oneself, and one would not regard their superiority as a deprivation. This seems quite reasonable to me. We also do not really envy, that is truly covet, something which is not within our reach. What affect us more closely are the things which seem to just elude our grasp—the things which are only just better than the things we have, and with which, therefore, we can compare them.

The range of *najar* is limited, therefore, by the nature of caste society, which accords a status to each group, and by the weakness of human imagination, which reduces the number of material desires to the scale of existing material goods. But clearly there are other human goods which are neither accorded by caste nor beyond the range of any human being to conceive, such as health, beauty, popularity and the like: to this extent all men are vulnerable to all men.

On the face of it this seems an absurd situation: it means that no one can enjoy the very simplest and common joys of life because of a constant anxiety that he is exciting the envy of someone else. Actually something like this can happen.

I was in another village, in the house of a relatively wealthy man who had been very good to me. I will call him Swāmidās because he was a devoted servant—*das*—of Swāmi Narāyan, the deified founder of a Gujarat sect. We were sitting outside his front door one evening, looking out on the small courtyard into which the door of a poorer kinsman's house also opened. After a pause in our conversation he suddenly voiced his train of thought and said, 'I *would* like to buy that house, but it's difficult.' 'But what on earth do you want it for, Swāmidās?' I asked. 'Well, you know, my children play out here, they play with the children from that house and it makes difficulties.' I remained silent. 'You see,' said Swāmidās, 'sometimes I give my boys something nice—like an apple from Bombay, and the other children see it and of course they would like an apple too.'

Swāmidās was dreaming out loud because there was no real likelihood that his kinsmen would sell their ancestral home. I do not think that, even if it had been possible, he would have forbidden his children to play with their cousins. He was far too generous a man to make his children secretive about the little luxuries he gave them. He was also far too sensible to allow himself to be forced into dispensing apples from Bombay to all the children in the neighbourhood. I never heard Swāmidās make a similar remark, and certainly he regarded beliefs about *najar* as ignorant superstitions. Nevertheless, he was expressing a real anxiety about his own affluence which was not large enough to cancel out the poverty of his children's playmates.

The sequel to the story about Surajben and her baby throws more light on the situation. Let me say something about her first. She was a tall, very fair woman, in her forties, but prematurely aged. She was, I think, rather conscious of her position as the wife of one of the most influential men in the village and a little over-concerned to stress her sensitivity in caste matters. I remember that she once told me how she had eaten at a railway station in a room where a Vaghari was present. The sight so upset her, she insisted, that she had been sick all the way home. The Vaghari are very low-caste herdsmen in Gujarat and the word has connotations of extreme filthiness. Surajben had five children, all boys. Her husband, Kishor, was a partner and manager of a small irrigation works owned by Swāmidās and some others who lived in a nearby village. The family had a financial security unknown to the bulk of the villagers. They ate rice every day and used wheat where the majority used millet. In short this was a family blessed in every way.

I had often spoken with Surajben about the beliefs and practices in which women were said to be the peculiar authorities. Amongst other things we had spoken of *najar* and she had explained a great deal to me. *Najar* was usually unconsciously exercised and sprang from desire. If one was contented one did not feel desire and therefore one's eyes could not hurt others. But there were some who had a kind of permanent core of envy in them amounting to a hatred, and such people could be recognized from their eyes which were unusually big and burning. If I observed Choto (8), for example, I would see what she meant. Choto had walked into the house one day when she was frying *bhajiān*, fritters; he had only glanced at the pan, but the whole batch was spoiled.

Choto was, in fact, a distant relative of her husband. They were both members of the same descent group and they were linked at the seventh inclusive generation. There is a saying in Gujarat to the effect that a distant cousin is a near relative when he is rich, but a poor brother is soon forgotten. The section of the lineage to which Choto belonged was extremely poor. Their area of the village was a crowded, dirty shanty town: Choto lived with his grandfather, his still unmarried sister, his mother, the uncle whom she had married after his father's death and the baby born of this marriage—all in a 'house' of two rooms, both of which would have fitted twice into Surajben's kitchen/dining-room.[3]

Choto's father and uncle had divided the property in the lifetime of the former; Choto now had a fragment of unirrigated land on which he grew chillies and a few other spices. His uncle/stepfather maintained the mother and baby himself on his own share—Choto could scarcely support his grandfather, his sister and himself from his land; he relied mainly upon his employment at the irrigation works. He was paid in cash and also in kind in that he had an occasional meal at Surajben's.

Here by any human understanding was a delicate situation. However, whereas Momad accepted patronage and, except in a few asides, showed no resentment, Choto burned. Momad was a Muslim and was treated as a member of a lower, but not polluting, caste. He was used to eating Surajben's food aside from the rest of the family, and to washing up his own utensils afterwards. Choto was of the same caste as Surajben, a Patidar, and as such could eat with the family. As a kinsman he had a right to be regarded as an equal. But he was to all intents and purposes a house servant as well as an employee of the husband.

Choto's father had been a rake and had died young, it was said, from drinking illicit liquor. Choto enjoyed something of his father's reputation. At night he told outrageous stories of his love affairs to the group of us who slept down by the irrigation works. These stories, like his ghost stories, were so enjoyably rich in exaggerated detail that no one ever challenged their veracity. He did have impressive eyes, large and glowing under thick eyebrows; he was not unaware of what Surajben said of their power.

On my second visit I got to know Choto quite well. Momad had gone to teach in a primary school some miles away. My Gujarati had much improved and Choto spoke no English. He was in touch with a side of village life very different from that represented by Surajben and her immediate family, and

I was made fully aware of their disapproval of this new friendship. With Choto I enjoyed the underworld of the village; whereas in Surajben's family I had learned how things should appear, with Choto I discovered a lot about how things are.

I employed Choto as my *sāthi*, my companion, and shortly afterwards he began to wear a black thread around his neck with a brass amulet attached. I never discovered whether this was to guard him against the envy of his new employment, or whether he spoke the truth when he said that it was because he had been ill. We spoke of *najar* one day and I mentioned the one case that I knew in some detail, that of Surajben's baby, Bhailal, and the suspicion that rested on Chiman.

Choto didn't let me finish my story. Chiman, so much older, was a friend of his. They went drinking together in the fields at night and Chiman knew how to cook the partridges that Choto occasionally killed.[4] 'That's stupid,' he said, 'why should Chiman look at Surajben's baby? His own brother's got several sons and they've none of them ever been sick. If Chiman were like that, that is where *najar* would have struck.' 'I am sorry,' I said, 'I thought you knew, and anyhow I just took it for granted that Surajben knew what she was at.' 'Surajben,' he almost spat the name out, 'she thinks of nothing but *najar*. I couldn't count the number of times she's called me out in the night to make some offering to the goddess— *mātāji* (see below, pp. 41 seq.), she's just mean that's all. Do you know I once dropped in when she was frying *bhajiān* and when she heard me coming she shoved the pan under a bed to hide it.' The implication was clear: had Choto found Surajben preparing *bhajiān* she would have been obliged to offer him some. I remembered Surajben's own account some three years earlier of what I assume was the same incident. 'It's the same with that whole damn family,' said Choto, 'their life is such, *najar* is bound to strike.'

Choto's view of things is complicated. He certainly

believed in *najar*, but had grounds to defend Chiman his friend from the accusation. *Najar* was not then the kind of innocent weakness I had supposed. There was an implication of a moral defect, short of conscious malice. Moreover it was attracted not by mere envy but by meanness and a refusal to share good things. That was Choto's opinion and this came close to making sense of *najar* to me. *Najar* situations came into being not simply when people had enjoyable qualities or goods, but when people having these things took pride in them, and enjoyed them, in some sense, as though they had deprived others of them. Thus a good-looking man would only be likely to accuse others of *najar* if he were himself vain.

GHOSTS

I mentioned earlier Choto's horrendous ghost stories and how they were met by a 'willing suspension of disbelief'. The villagers enjoy frightening themselves with ghost stories: the taste seems universal. The young also indulge in elaborate practical jokes. There's a man in Sundarana now in his sixties, a Bareia by caste, who told me how, years ago, Kishor, Surajben's husband, and some others rigged up an oil lamp and an old *dhoti* in a thorn bush near his home in such a manner that it popped up moaning every time he tried to enter the lane. He stayed out in the fields petrified and cold all night. This had happened when they were in their late teens, at a time of life when inter-caste friendships were still possible, and a certain laxity over the rules of caste was tolerated so long as it was concealed. If marriage does not naturally induce responsibility in these matters, the marital status imposes it.

The old man who told me the story, together with Choto and his audience, believed nevertheless in ghosts at an altogether more disturbing level. The old man told me once, after a night of story-telling in which he had fully participated, that Choto was a shocking liar of course, but all the

same it was not good to tell such stories because they could
bring about the very horrors that they described. There were
certain parts of the village, outside the residential area, where
no man in his right mind would ever walk alone. Collective
representations are often contagious and affect even the
outsider. I certainly could not avoid a sense of uneasy tension
when I had occasion to walk in the vicinity of such places at
night.

The general word for ghost is *bhut* and the word connotes
a terrifying ugliness, but not necessarily malevolence. Many
ghosts are feminine and may still be called *bhut*, but
bhutadi, a diminutive form, designates a female spirit. The
word *bhut* is interesting; it derives from the Sanskrit notion
of existence and the continuity of being and can have this
meaning still in Gujarati literature. *Bhutkal* means past time,
kal meaning time or period, or, in grammar, the past tense.
Bhutmātra is the totality of being; *bhutdāya*, compassion for
all beings, and so on. The use of the word *bhut* to mean
horrendous ghosts is a special development.

Among the *bhut* there are special kinds. There is the *zan*
(from the Arabic *djin*); this is the spirit of a man versed in
the evil arts *meli vidhya* (literally dirty science); there is
also the *bakrākshas*—the ghost of a Brahman. But apart from
the word *bhut* itself the very commonest is *chudel*. The
chudel is the spirit of a woman. Unlike all other *bhut* her
appearance is seductively beautiful. A man might meet such
a woman in the fields and could only know his peril from the
fact that her feet pointed backwards. In a country where the
women wear the *sāri* down to their feet this deformity might
well go unnoticed, but even so, the stories have it, the *chudel*
is so utterly beautiful that men have been knowingly seduced
and as a result of sleeping with her, reduced to impotence
for the rest of their lives.

Ghosts are most usually feared when they inhabit the fields.
The few who enter houses are more manageable and sometimes even benign. The phenomena reported are rather like

those attributed to poltergeists among ourselves; they throw pots, clothes and furniture without harming human beings. There is, for example, a Muslim house in Sundarana which was infested in this way about a hundred years ago. The *bhut* began its activities by hurling down bricks from the wall. It is said that a Patidar neighbour, who was called in to witness this, observed, characteristically, that there would be a good deal more sense in the situation if the spirit were to throw down gold, whereupon, on that one occasion, a shower of gold descended. This spirit is still said to be active occasionally.

Some house ghosts go as far as to possess their victims in such a way that they destroy their own property. The only help is to buy a charm, preferably of iron. In general it is believed that iron makes any ghost burst into flames and disappear. This does not always work. There was a man in Sundarana who had a house built by the local carpenter but did not pay his bill. The carpenter died and possessed the house owner so that the man went mad and destroyed his own house. No iron charm would work and so it was concluded that the carpenter had been a secret adept in the evil art and had become a *zan*. If a possessing spirit can be persuaded to speak through its victim and express its grievance, and if this grievance can be met, then it will usually go away in peace.

Grievance is common to all these manifestations of the dead even though some are nameless and the grievance is not known. It is simply assumed that they are consumed by some unidentifiable regret. Most often, however, the regret relates to the known obligations of others which have not been fulfilled, such as the carpenter's unpaid bill. More generally the grievance may derive from unfulfilled desire. There was a field in Sundarana haunted by the *bhut* of a man who had owned an adjoining field. He had maintained, throughout his life, an acrimonious border dispute with his neighbour, which he had finally lost. The *chudel* is said to be the spirit of a woman who died childless; her revenge is appropriate just as her regret can never be assuaged. It is interesting that, in a society in which women are usually blamed for a sterile marriage, impotence strikes the man who copulates with this spirit. There is a kind of justice in the folklore.

It is not difficult to understand that this belief in an unfulfilled desire relates closely to the belief in *najar*. Just as I will fear the envious evil eye only if I am aware of my own greed, and vanity is only a form of greed, so will I only fear the activity of ghosts if I have a guilty conscience. Many villagers said that to be unafraid was the best protection of all, and this is what the old man was getting at when he said that ghost stories were dangerous. Fear generates the profounder guilt to which a general belief relates, just as specific guilt relates to the belief in a specific ghost. I never heard that spirits were restless because of some ritual inadequacy in the funeral ceremonies. With the exception of the *chudel* all cases related to unpaid debts, land disputes, or vows unaccomplished, that is to say, things which the living might remedy with the family or kin of the deceased.

Some ghosts only require feeding from time to time, usually by a peepul tree. This food is taken at night by someone who does not look behind him, either coming or going. Such ghosts, together with those who regularly inhabit houses and those who possess people, come close to incorporation in the permanent pantheon of the village. There was one such permanent ghost site in Sundarana where food was left regularly and a lamp given occasionally. Some spoke of the ghost there as a *mātā*, a kind of goddess about which we shall hear more later, and also as the spirit of the great-grandmother of a man in the village. We shall see that a development from ghost to goddess is not impossible. All that is needed is more trouble associated with the spot, and a greater attention consequently paid to it, for others to start venerating the place. This is not hypothetical. Elsewhere in Gujarat, particularly Saurashtra, the spirits of women who have committed suttee, and even those who have proved themselves otherwise to be true *sati*—chaste and virtuous models of wifely behaviour—are deified under the general term *mātā*, although their immediate descendants continue to distinguish them as *sati*.

The reader who has some knowledge of Indian beliefs might well ask at this point: 'What about reincarnation, transmigration or re-birth? If Hindus have such beliefs how can they at the same time believe in ghosts?' To this I could add that the villagers also have beliefs about heaven and hell, more particularly the latter. One afternoon a young man was sitting by me as I was resting in a darkened room. He was very kindly ridding the room of flies by snatching them out of the air as he sat. I congratulated him on his practised ease. 'It's nothing,' he said, and then with a slightly worried look, 'but I sometimes worry about all that walking, walking, walking.' It was altogether too hot to press the matter at that time; it later emerged that he was speaking of hell, a hell in which man is obliged to walk on and on for ever and alone. On the other hand the belief in re-birth according to the law of *karma* was occasionally expressed, and there was even a little ritual about it connected with funeral ceremonies. The night after a cremation the women would spread flour on the floor, cover it with a sieve and leave a lighted lamp on top of the sieve to burn all night. In the morning they said that they could discern in the flour the footprint of the creature into which the departed soul had entered. This was not a universal or in any way mandatory practice, and indeed it was dismissed by some men as a foolish superstition. A far more regular institution was the throwing out of food, curds and water, most often on the anniversary of a death. It was believed that if the crows took this food it would in some way benefit the departed soul. I never saw the crows pay any attention to these offerings nor did I ever see anyone wait to see whether they would.

The villagers of Sundarana, like the majority of peoples

known to social anthropologists, were very vague about the after-life. I suspect that much of the information collected from different parts of the world on such matters is more often synthesized on the spot, in response to Western query, rather than the integrated theory that is sometimes presented in the works of anthropologists. When Indian peasants, or philosophers for that matter, are confronted with the ancient 'contradiction' between a belief in individual survival in hell or as a ghost on the one hand, or on the other the belief in re-birth, they can very easily sythesize the two beliefs: death is followed by a period of punishment or reward which varies in length according to merit, but ultimately the law of *karma* requires a re-birth unless the soul has been freed for ever from the operation of that law.

I do not think it very sensible to give in to a desire to solve contradictions in this way, and I find support for this view from village conversation. For the social anthropologist it is not only a question of *what* is said, but *who* says it and to *whom* and *where*. Thinking over remarks about the after-life in this way it seems clear to me that there is a rather simple formula underlying this 'contradiction' in beliefs. Re-birth is primarily for other people. Just as few Westerners accept fully the finiteness of their own existence, so that death tends to be thought of as something that happens to others, so the Gujarati peasants when they speak of themselves as individuals conceive of a hell or some sort of heaven. It is when they speak of others, when they are looking for some wider theory to explain the grief, sorrow and misfortune of others, that they have recourse to the theory of re-birth. Certainly they do not deny salvation to others, equally they apply the re-birth theory to their own occasional griefs but primarily the emphases are distributed as I have described.

There is another aspect of the matter. It seems clear in some contexts that actually these two beliefs are not at the same level. The belief in some kind of eternal salvation relates to the future whereas the belief in re-birth relates to the past.

Some sin in a previous life 'explains' why a man is born as an untouchable, or why some woman has had the great misfortune to survive her husband, and is obliged to live out the inauspicious life of a widow.

Let me conclude with a summary note on *najar* and beliefs about ghosts. Both are clearly related to human obligations and the failure to meet them. Joyce Cary in *The Horse's Mouth*, talking of the secretive way in which tramps in a London doss-house cook their food, speaks of the 'evil eye which is the eye of envy'. Certainly, at one level, the belief in *najar* tells us something about the greed and avarice which can only be found in their purest form where people live on the bread-line, have never lived anywhere else, and do not expect anything more. It also tells of the acute value placed upon the, for us, ephemeral goods of youth, good looks and vitality in a population where the average expectation of life is only thirty years, where women are soon prematurely senile, and young men show signs of muscle wastage at twenty-five.

At the level of the sociological, *najar* tells us of status and equality. *Najar* is not to be feared between equals, such as brothers, nor between people whose status is clearly different and defined. It is most to be feared when those who should be equal are not so in fact. From this point of view natural good looks, which might be the gift of all, may be envied by any. At the social level, however, *najar* bites deepest within the caste, especially in a large caste such as the Patidar, where, in one lineage, a man may live in contentment while his kinsman spends his life near to starvation. When some do accumulate wealth, the fear of *najar* defines the ways in which wealth may be enjoyed, that is with modesty; it requires all men to be generous according to their means.

The evil eye can be turned away, and its ill effects can be cured. The belief in ghosts speaks more of irremediable ills past, and of unavoidable evil in life itself. The wilful over-looker who is the embodiment of pure unmotivated malice, the practitioner of the black science and the barren woman—for these there are no remedies. Among the ghosts are also those who have been cheated of their dues just as, in a sense, the barren woman is cheated. Such beliefs underlie the value of a good death which leaves neither material nor moral debt or loan behind it.

NOTES

1. The name is a corruption of Mohammad. Momad is one of a small group of Muslims in the village known as Vora. This name is a corruption of Bohora, the name of a large Shia Muslim sect. The corruption of the name is symptomatic of these village Muslims' ignorance of their faith. They circumcise their male children and visit the mosque in town once or twice a year, at which time they also eat meat. For the most part they behave as a vegetarian caste of middling status and are so regarded by the Hindus.

2. J. C. Pratt, who has done field-work in Siena, draws my attention to an over-simplification here. He points out that sickness can also be caused by excessive love, *volere troppo bene*; as he puts it, 'we have to take jealousy into account as well as envy'. This suggestion from the Italian material that jealousy, or possessiveness, can directly harm its object must be explored in future comparative studies. (J. C. Pratt, D.Phil. thesis.)

3. The re-marriage of the widow by a younger brother of the deceased is an economical custom much condemned by people of good family and pretension. Choto's family was looked down upon by those who had relinquished this custom within living memory. Choto's sister, although past the age at which village girls are usually married, still shamefacedly wears the blouse and skirt of a maiden.

4. The Patidar are in principle vegetarian, but meat-eating is not unthinkable. The fact to note is that a man might eat meat, or drink alcohol, out in the fields; he would not dream of bringing such things home to pollute the house. Similarly, a man might have sexual intercourse with an Untouchable woman, but he would not take food or water at her hands.

3

Goddess Cults—Status and Change

In this chapter I reverse the order of what I believe to be a historical development. I describe three ceremonies performed in Patidar households on one and the same night, all ostensibly for the same purpose, but each one telling us of the standing of the various groups. I go on to generalize and to show how whole castes vary their ceremonies according to their view of their own status or their hopes for the regard of others. The line of development in both cases seems to be from a state of symbiosis between pure and impure castes to a more univocal dependence upon Brahmanic values only.

I then turn to the past to describe an older cult where this symbiotic relationship is fully acknowledged; a cult which has faded in this part of Gujarat, but which is still active further west. The breakdown of the ritual interdependence of the pure and impure castes seems to me to be of immense significance, foreshadowing as it does the breakdown of political and economic interdependence between caste and caste.

I have mentioned *mātā* several times, but what are they? The word means, on the face of it, 'honoured mother', but the word *mātā* is not used in everyday speech for mother. Indeed, when I say it *means* 'honoured mother' I am relying on a dictionary, and the Sanskrit word *mātr*, a mother. I never heard a villager develop an imagery of motherhood in connexion with this word similar to that our own clergy make when they try to explain why we speak of God the Father. As a matter of fact, the dictionary comes nearer to peasant usage when, as a secondary meaning for *mātā,* it gives 'smallpox'. We shall see that the actual beliefs and practices which revolve around the word make any easy translation impossible.

Sundarana, like all villages in Gujarat, has an uncountable number of shrines associated with *mātā.* Sometimes these are thorn bushes and one can only know that the *mātā* is sitting there, as the villagers put it, by the rags tied to their branches. People tear off a bit of their clothing and tie it on as a votive offering. A much more common sight is that of two simple bricks lying flat, about six inches apart, with a little clay dish between them, sheltered by a third brick transversely resting on the other two. Not quite so common, but familiar enough to any traveller, is the *deri* or *daheri,* a small domed shrine of plastered brick, not much above three feet high. There is an arched opening on one side and most often the shrine is entirely empty. Sometimes one can find a debris of little clay dishes inside and on the surrounding earth, sometimes a chaplet of coconuts has been slung round the dome and empty shells of coconuts are littered around. In a very few cases one can find crude figures of horses made of clay or rag.

The clay dishes are to contain the commonest votive offering, a lamp. Oil or *ghi,* clarified butter, is put in the dish and a small cotton wick is floated on the surface. A more substantial offering is the coconut, while the horse figures are a speciality of certain *mātā.* The horse is their *vāhan,* literally their vehicle, the creature on which they ride. All these offerings are either to placate or to thank. A woman has lost her goat and promises the *mātā* a lamp if she finds it before nightfall. Surajben has had a bad dream and wakes up one of the boys sleeping in the courtyard to send a lamp to the *mātā*—immediately.

There are still other beings referred to as *mātā* who have

temples with images and resident priests, but such buildings, naturally enough, are not found in the villages although the *mātā* concerned may still be so. There is, for example, the famous temple of Ambājimātā on Mount Abu in Gujarat where the *mātā* sits, but she can also sit in the house of a devotee; in a shrine in a field; or, indeed, anywhere that she fancies. The pattern is one familiar to the Roman tradition in Christianity: our Lady of Lourdes, or Fatima, has one chosen spot associated with her, and is also worshipped in thousands of households.

The connexion between Ambājimātā on Mount Abu and Ambājimātā in the fields is obvious to the peasants, but there are other *mātā* in the village who also have central and famous sites about which they know nothing. Again, there are nameless *mātā*. The behaviour of the villagers to all of these is uniform and it seems best, therefore, to look at *mātā* beliefs from their point of view, at least to start with.

As I have suggested the *mātā* are part of everyday life, but they also have their special season, *navarātri,* the Nine Nights in the first, or bright, half of the month of Ashvin, the last month in the lunar calendar. The celebrations culminate on the eighth night, *mahāstmi,* the Great Eighth.[1]

On one *mahāstmi* I attended three ceremonies, and I now describe the events which occurred, together with the revealing differences between them.

The first ceremony was in Shivabhai's house and was attended by his immediate kin and a few friends, Choto and myself included. Shivabhai was a mild rather ineffectual character, a member of a very small and poor lineage in the village. The celebration in his house was of relatively recent institution. The *mātā* in whose honour we were assembling had originally been nameless, and her place had survived in one of Shivabhai's fields; who had originally set up her shrine no one could remember. Shivabhai had encouraged her, and I say this deliberately because there are many ruined and forgotten shrines which are almost totally neglected. People put a lamp by them during the Nine Nights just to be on the safe side, but for the rest of the year they forget about them. Shivabhai, anyhow, had built a small shrine of bricks for the nameless *mātā*, and planted trees about it. Some time after this, he said, she possessed him one night, revealed her name, Vāhanvati—and asked him to take her into his house. Shivabhai had thus become, in the last few years, the *bhuvo*, devotee-priest, of this *mātā*, and had established a minor reputation for cures.

One hears so much about Brahmans as priests in India that one is very often led to conclude that they are the only priests. In fact, the number of people having the kind of office that we would translate as 'priesthood' in a village like Sundarana is probably greater than that of Brahmans resident in the village. The priest of any godling or *mātā* can in theory be of any caste. However, they are very rarely of higher caste and, in Sundarana, I think that Shivabhai was the only *bhuvo* among the Patidar. The majority were of lower caste. Such priests might be called *pujāri*, that is someone who, like a Brahman, performs the *pujā*, worship. More commonly, however, he is called *bhuvo*, a word derived from a Sanskrit name for Shiva, *bhav*. The distinctive function of the *bhuvo* is to become possessed, at which time he trembles and speaks with the voice of the *mātā* to complain of neglect, to ask for offerings, and to make promises and predictions. I will describe a typical scene shortly. Although the *mātā* normally possesses her chief servant, her *bhuvo*, she may seize on any-one present to a greater or lesser degree by simply making them tremble, or by speaking through them. At a big ceremony it is quite common to see half a dozen men jerking up and down while the main procession is in progress.

The trembling, nodding head and the querulous speech of the *bhuvo* when possessed is a favourite subject for village mimics who may regard all *bhuvo* as bogus but continue to believe in the act of possession. Such imitations are regarded as slightly dangerous since they have been known to result in genuine possessions. Given the beliefs this is not surprising, for the rapid deep breathing which precedes the possession can produce a peculiar state of dissociation.

On the Eighth Night that I am talking about we were invited to eat at Shivabhai's house. He had been fasting from the first day of the Nine Nights but, apart from the fact that he did not eat with us, he played the host with normal cheerfulness. I should add that his fast, *upvās*, limited him to taking tea twice a day and to one meal of *suran*, a large, shapeless root vegetable known as Elephant's Foot.

After we had eaten and washed our hands we went up a ladder into a small room upstairs where we sat facing a small shrine constructed for the occasion out of silver and coloured paper. Above it hung four pictures depicting scenes from the life of the Lord Krishna. The shrine itself was empty. After a little while Shiva joined us carrying a broken tile on which were some burning coals. On to these coals he threw a little incense which he offered in front of the shrine where, I was told, the *mātā* was already sitting. He then turned to face his small congregation and wafted the scented smoke towards us. After this he put the tile down at the side of the shrine and called for a knife. He was given one of the small clasp knives such as are used for preparing vegetables in the kitchen. Sitting cross-legged with this in his hand, he went suddenly into a violent convulsion, clearly straining his stomach and neck muscles and breathing deep and fast. After about thirty seconds he snatched at a fresh lime and hacked it roughly into pieces which he threw about the room; in all he disposed of four limes in the course of the session. Then, an old woman, his elder brother's wife, questioned the *mātā*: '*Mā*, why isn't my baby [one of her grandchildren] getting any better?' Shivabhai shrieked, increased his convulsions and then began muttering unintelligibly to himself. Finally he said 'Bring the child.' The baby was brought and, still twitching and muttering, Shiva laid his hand on its head. He called for red string and a bundle of this was given to him.

He tossed it into the air, played with it and finally threw it down violently in front of the old woman saying: 'Tie this.' One of the threads was teased out from the bundle and taken away, the rest was put down by the side of the shrine for retail later to other mothers in need. Shiva then went back into his convulsions, groanings and deep breathings. After a while he said, peevishly, 'Ask, ask. Why don't you ask?' One of the boys laughed and said, 'Well, go on someone, ask. I don't know how to, you've got to have the knack.' There was silence apart from Shiva's breathing but slowly questions began to come, the questioners addressing Shivabhai variously as Mahārāj, a term normally used to a Brahman, Mā, Bā and Mātāji. In between questions, or during the convulsions, we chatted quite freely amongst ourselves, as though we were sitting waiting for a train, and only fell silent at the more dramatic moments. Someone, I think it was Choto, asked about a recent theft (from myself), and two boys of lower caste, who were not present, were named by the *mātā*. Choto, who knew very well that some people had accused him of the theft, called on all to witness what the *mātā* had said. Another man asked whether his wife, who had run off to Ahmedabad, would return to him. Shiva replied that it would be an expensive matter, various offerings would have to be made. The man said 'Where?' and was told 'Here, of course.' After specifying the details Shiva extended his palm, for all the world as though he were doing a deal in the market place, and said *'Kabul'* agreed? and the questioner slapped the open palm in confirmation. *'Kabul.'*

Throughout the proceedings very little reverence was shown to the *mātā* or to her medium. The conventional tone of the *bhuvo* is that of a peevish old woman, and that of the questioners an affectionate tolerance. One question, relating to the fields, received an unsatisfactory reply. Two or three people laughed and said, 'Well, we knew that.' The *bhuvo* snapped back, 'Then what did you ask for?'

In the course of the session, which I suppose lasted a little over an hour, various *mātā* took over the medium, and as his behaviour changed members of the audience asked 'Who are you?' The most dramatic appearance was reserved for the end when the *bhuvo* snatched up a rusty and blunt old sword from the shrine and, pressing its edge on to his tongue with both hands, sucked vigorously at the blood which was supposed to be flowing: Kalika had come. Kalika is another name for Kāli, a ferocious and bloodthirsty goddess worshipped in many parts of India.

The whole proceeding ended abruptly. Shiva suddenly relaxed and appeared exhausted. The company got up and left, folding their hands to the shrine as they passed it saying, '*Jāy mātāji*, hail to the *mātā*.'

During the whole performance Shivabhai's actions, when looking for things, taking them up or giving them, seemed entirely controlled. The place where he was squatting was perilously close to the open trap-door leading to the room below. My comment, and my use of the word 'performance', is in harmony with the attitude of the company as we gathered in the street below. No one believed that the whole thing was a sham, equally no one seemed to feel that it was convincing in every detail. The general reaction seemed to belong to the twilight world of superstition between faith and knowledge. One man summed it up after having voiced his own doubts and said, 'Still, one never knows, there's probably something in it.' Other people in the village were more frankly sceptical and regarded Shivabhai's cult as a trick to get money. Some women, however, consulted him regularly.

From Shivabhai's house we strolled on to the next ceremony which was held in the front room of a large house in the densest area of Patidar concentration in the village. This was not a private affair such as the one we had just witnessed; it was something much more on behalf of a whole lineage, the Prabhudas Lakhujivalla. There were, however, members of other Patidar lineages present, and members of other castes. This was an annual event and something of a spectacle. This time the shrine itself was not on view; it was a permanent one in the inner room from which such things as the *bhuvo* called for were brought. The *bhuvo* was a man of low caste, a Patanwadia, and, although many people put questions to the *bhuvo* in the course of the evening, the leading part in the questioning was taken by a man of the Rāval caste, a caste associated with music-making, particularly on the drums.

The whole performance was more polished and, so to speak, professional than the one we had just witnessed. The *bhuvo* sat quietly chatting with the Rāval and then fell silent, as did the majority of the audience. The presence of a *mātā* became evident from the twitching of the *bhuvo*'s muscles and face; he finally moved into full possession and announced himself as Ambājimātā, upon which the audience started singing a hymn in honour of the goddess as the *bhuvo* started to twitch. Ambāji was followed by Kalika who, on this occasion, did nothing spectacular; she was followed by other *mātā*. There were no particularly vigorous convulsions nor any violence. The traditional tone was, however, maintained. The *bhuvo*, once in his trance, spoke with a high, peevish, quavering tone. As the hymn drew to its close he was heard muttering to himself sarcastically, 'Very nice, very pleasant. I know you lot, you're going to do this, you're going to do that, but you don't do anything. You leave me alone, you don't feed me. Why should I have anything to do with you?' and so on. The Rāval made it his business to cajole the *mātā* into a more pleasant frame of mind. This dialogue was engrossing and it was quite easy to forget that one was listening to two grown men. The Rāval, half solicitous, half joking, spoke exactly as though to a much loved but tiresome old grandmother. 'Come, come, don't talk like that. Look at all these people who've come to see you. Look at all these nice presents we've brought you,' and so on. As regards promises of cures and predictions for the coming year, the proceedings were much as before. At one point the *bhuvo* was asked about the child who was not recovering despite treatments. He replied that it was no affair of the *mātā*, nor *najar*, nor the activity of some *bhut*. The questioner quite blankly contradicted him and said that another *mātā* had, through her *bhuvo*, claimed that the sickness had resulted from the neglect of her shrine. At this challenge the Rāval called for a pot and a handful of grain and the *mātā* was asked to say, rather as in a table-tapping seance, whether an equal number of grains should signify yes or no. Then positive and negative questions were asked about the source of the child's sickness. After each question a small quantity of grain which the Rāval counted was thrown on to a cloth. In this way a diagnosis and treatment of the sickness were arrived at.

For me this session was particularly noteworthy for two reasons. First of all the *mātā*, through her *bhuvo*, kept demanding liquid opium but was given instead a hookah to smoke and occasionally water sweetened with sugar. Secondly, on one occasion she demanded, with some vehemence, a goat. This request was met with laughter mingled, as far as I could judge, with embarrassment. The Rāval said: 'Ah no, don't ask that. What do you want with a goat?' And the *bhuvo* abandoned the request immediately. These requests were interesting because the drinking of opium and the eating of meat of any sort are regarded as low-caste practices to which no Patidar would, especially in public, admit. We shall see later the significance of the request.

By the time this second session had finished it was getting on for eleven o'clock at night, and I was thinking of my bed. Choto had slipped off somewhere when one of Surajben's young cousins came up to tell me that I, and a few others, had been called to another house. The house was, I discovered, that of Hāthi, the wealthiest man in the Vallabhvalla section of the Prabhudās Lakhujivalla lineage, which regarded itself as superior to other sections. The timing of the ceremony was nevertheless tactful. This group of 'secessionists' had taken care to avoid any appearance of a deliberate clash of

E

programmes and, indeed, most of them had attended the second ceremony.

The third ceremony was altogether more exclusive than either of the other two that I had attended that night. Apart from myself, only families in this one lineage section were represented. The courtyard was brightly lit with paraffin pressure lamps, and the ceremony centred on a *daheri* which had been specially whitewashed and painted for the occasion. The chief *mātā*, on this occasion, was said to be the same Kalika who had appeared twice earlier in the evening. But this time the element of possession had been eliminated entirely. There was no *bhuvo* and instead a Brahman had been called to perform *homa*, an orthodox fire service, with offerings of *ghi*, wheat and rice. After the sacrifice, a lamp of *ghi*, incense and *kanku*, a red paste, were offered on a dish to the fire while the names of famous gods, well known in Indian literature, were recited. When that was completed the dish was offered up to the shrine while the names of the famous goddesses of literature were recited, the litany concluded with, 'and all other gods'. The dish with its offerings was then placed within the shrine. Using the *kanku* the Brahman marked the walls by the shrine with a swastika and *trisul*, the sign of a trident, then all the company received at his hand a *kanku* on their brow and the proceedings came to an end. The general atmosphere on this occasion was quite different from either of the two preceding ceremonies. Whereas before the audience had sat chatting and laughing and had felt as free to make jokes about the *mātā* as about each other, here I felt myself to be in a much more 'religious' situation. There was no chatting during the ceremony, people sat formally and concentrated upon the Brahman's activities with serious faces. After the Brahman had wrapped up his utensils and gone, the host continued to sit with a solemn face and we, in turn, took leave of him in the most formal manner. It was now near midnight and *mahāstmi* had come to its close.

All the *mātā* involved in these ceremonies have two things in common which distinguish them from other *mātā* in the village; they are house-dwelling and non-specialized, by which I mean that they are not associated with any particular activity. Several *mātā* in the village, together with one male godling, Bhattiji, are specifically associated with particular diseases of which the most feared, in the past especially, is Sitalamata, the smallpox *mātā*. The word *sital* here means 'cool' and, because the smallpox burns the skin, this is a very polite name for the goddess who is said to be hot tempered and easily insulted. Another specialist is Hadakāimātā (from *hadakavā*, hydrophobia). This *mātā* is in most villages located in the Untouchable quarter and her *bhuvo* is also an Untouchable. The dogs which infest the Untouchable quarter are usually said to be more fierce than other dogs in the village because, people believe, they eat more meat. Both of these diseases are less to be feared now than they were in the past. In Sundarana I heard little of them and would probably have heard nothing about Hadakāimātā had I not made inquiries. In the fields about a quarter of a mile away from the residential area of Sundarana there is quite a large shrine, about nine feet high, dedicated to Joganiomata. This again must have been an important place in the past. It is set in a piece of ground surrounded by a wall enclosing a ruined *dharmsālā*, a resting place for pilgrims, said to have been built many years ago by a wealthy Bania, a member of one of Gujarat's trading castes, who lost and found his purse at that spot. Today the *mātā* is looked after by an elderly *bhuvo* who is paid by Surajben's husband, Kishor. It seems that in the past some kind of ordeal was held here when a crime was suspected, but today the place is neglected, as the incumbent *bhuvo* bitterly complains.

Of all the specialists it is the male godling Bhattiji who still maintains popularity. He is the only male in the local pantheon but is found in other villages with Baliadev, the consort of the smallpox *mātā*. Bhattiji is associated with snakes and scorpions, and the different ways in which the association can be viewed tell us a great deal about beliefs in Gujarat.

When I first came across a Bhattiji shrine it was in the fields near a predominantly Jain Bania village. Many Bania in Gujarat are members of the Jain sect and, in orthodox families, they obey the precepts of that sect which minimize the possibilities of violence to any living creature. Here I was told that Bhattiji was the guardian of snakes and scorpions and would, as a punishment, possess anyone who killed one of these creatures, until he had made amends. In Sundarana, on the other hand, where the *bhuvo* of Bhattiji was of the Bareia caste, who have no such scruples, I was told that of course such creatures must be killed, and that Bhattiji was the protector of men. Anyone bitten by a snake must have immediate recourse to his shrine where an enormous drum is kept to summon the *bhuvo*, at any time of the night or day, to administer the cure. I shall have more to say about Bhattiji and his shrine in another connexion. Here it is sufficient to note that so long as any *mātā*, or godling, has specialist associations with any particular disease or mishap, he or she does not take up permanent abode in any house.

I said earlier that Shivabhai had 'encouraged' a *mātā* who was apparently quiescent in his fields. The way in which she entered his house was typical. When a man falls sick of general debility, or of fever which he cannot shake off, then supernatural causes are looked for while physical treatment continues. If the possibility of *najar* has been eliminated then a *bhuvo* is called. In such a case one would not call the *bhuvo* of a specialized or named *mātā*—that would be to prejudge the issue. A devotee of some nameless or (which is the same thing) multi-named *mātā* is called. He invites possession by the *mātā*, and that *mātā* who is troubling the man will, perhaps after the intervention of others, eventually speak and say why she has brought the disease.

In some cases she may simply specify a remedy in the way

of an offering, but in others she may express the desire to come and sit in the house. A shrine is then prepared for her which may be anything from a design on the wall to a glass-fronted cupboard with pictures of Kāli or Ambāji in it. This *mātā* may then give no further trouble, so long as she receives daily attention. The householder may or may not, according to his economic condition and piety, call a *bhuvo* once a year to be possessed by the *mātā* and be fed on her behalf. There are many house *mātā* in Sundarana which remain apparently quiescent for years in this way. When the house-holder dies, then the son who inherits that part of the house in which the *mātā* is sitting will attend to her. If there is no trouble the attentions which the *mātā* receives become more perfunctory as time goes by; storage pots and boxes accumulate in front of the shrine and finally, in the course of making repairs, re-plastering the wall or extending a room, the *mātā* is lost to sight. Sometimes people are troubled by a *mātā* who claims that she was venerated by an ancestor and has been neglected. If the shrine is in a cupboard it stands more chance of permanence but, in such circumstances, it will very rapidly be assimilated with the picture of Kāli or Ambāji; soon this itself becomes only a background for the brass or stone images of more widely known deities of the Hindu pantheon, bought at various places of pilgrimage.

A *mātā* may, at the particular wish of a devotee, be transferred from one family to another, temporarily or permanently. The householder himself, or a *bhuvo*, becomes possessed and offers a coconut to the goddess which is afterwards placed in the hands of the applicants. If the applicant trembles, the *mātā* has inhabited the coconut and may be carried to her new place. In one instance a man disputed the ownership of a piece of land with another and paid a *bhuvo* to 'seat' his *mātā* on the disputed property, to trouble his opponent. The intention here was that the *mātā* would further his interests and hamper his rival who was in fact in possession. The rival pointed out the shrine to me with great amusement. The *mātā* can also be evicted. In Sundarana a carpenter bought a house in which Kalikamātā was found to be sitting. He belonged to the Swāmi Narāyan sect, which I have already mentioned. As a devout member of the sect he did not wish to perpetuate the cult of the *mātā*. He himself did not believe in the *mātā*, he said, but to save appearances the *mātā* was transferred to a coconut by which *pujā* was performed. The coconut was then reverently thrown into a nearby river. The iron flail with which the former *bhuvo* had lashed himself when possessed—this is a habit with some—the carpenter kept, 'It's handy to beat the wife with.'

However, in a few families, and those mostly of the Patidar caste, the cult of the *mātā* is preserved and even expanded in the second generation. The *mātā* of the second ceremony that I attended is said to have been seated there by the founder of the lineage, Prabhudās Lakhuji himself. The Patidar of that lineage liked to refer to it as a *kuldevi*, literally the lineage goddess. This term connotes prestige; in most parts of Gujarat only Brahmans and the royally connected Rajputs have such lineage goddesses. Although such claims are made by some Patidar families in some villages, the practice is by no means universal and, I suspect, is to be understood as yet another attempt to associate the family of the claimant with high status.

In his particular case the claim also served another purpose. Those who attended the third ceremony were attempting to dissociate themselves from their poorer kinsmen, and it was these latter who particularly insisted that the *mātā* of Prabhudās Lakhuji was the *mātā* of the entire lineage, including the seceding group, and therefore its *kuldevi*. The seceding group certainly and explicitly repudiated this claim. In general it was rare to find a *mātā* who had been in receipt of continuous worship in one house for many generations.

The reference in the preceding paragraph to status-seeking by imitation of practices thought to be superior is a feature of our own society as much as of caste society. What are the differences between us and them in this? The main difference is that this kind of imitation amongst ourselves is more the affair of an individual; in India it is a group matter. Secondly, whereas in our own society there are various ladders which a man may aspire to climb, in traditional Indian society there is only one, and that is determined by the values of caste. The behaviour of the local Brahmans constitutes largely the scale of these values, so that if, as is most often the case, the local Brahmans are vegetarian, then vegetarianism is a local caste value: people who imitate the Brahmans in this matter are that much more highly regarded than those who do not. Today, of course, with the growth of literacy and the accompanying spread of literature, notions of respectable behaviour derived from temples, monasteries and the centres of wide-spread sects, increasingly affect these local ideals. Today it is quite likely that although meat (but never beef) eating is tolerated in a certain area by higher castes, a lower caste may attach itself to the vegetarian scale.[2] In general, while all men want to be rich, powerful and the like, riches and power must be, so to speak, invested in the values of caste if they are to bring status.

But, and here is another major difference, wealth is not freely converted into status as happens, if slowly, amongst ourselves. Caste society imposes limits and what these are can be seen from the following true account.

There are two villages near Sundarana—I prefer not to name them and shall refer to them as A and B—which had been rivals for years. Both are prosperous and have con-nexions with government, industry, high commerce and the like. What the original dispute was no one really knows, but people say it was over a marriage and this is certainly very likely in this part of India. Whatever it may have been, there are apparent grounds for rivalry in the present. I call them villages but in the census one is classified as a town and both have substantial populations. If the government sets up a secondary school in the area it must be in one of these two.

The other, which contributes a large proportion of the student population, must watch its children walk the two miles to school. Again, a very bitter dispute arose over the question as to which village should have the railway connexion. Whereas before, Patidar land-owners, like their British counterparts in the past, fought initially to keep the railways off valuable agricultural land, today relatively swift contact with the cities is more prized, and to be on the railway has obvious commercial advantages.

The particular squabble that I am going to describe is of the kind that can only arise when rivalry is entrenched, and almost anything can be the subject of a row. In this case it was a clock-tower! The men of A had put up a fine clock-tower, visible and audible for quite a distance in this flat countryside. The men of B were determined to have a bigger and better one. As all too often happens, disputes arose within village B about who had subscribed, who had not, how much this man should give and so on. In the midst of this stalemate one man, a native of B, now a wealthy cloth merchant in Bombay, offered to foot the entire bill. The Patidar of B were now in a quandary because this wealthy benefactor happened to be an Untouchable. The mean and arrogant solution to their predicament was this: yes, the Untouchable could be allowed to pay for the clock-tower, but he would not be allowed to have his name inscribed as donor on the foundation stone. Since most foundation stones of schools, *dharmsala*, temples and hospitals tend to have a list inscribed on them not only of the subscribers but also, often enough, the amount of money which each has given, the Untouchable withdrew his offer and left the Patidar to their problem. In short, an Untouchable, however wealthy and even respected in commercial circles he may be, cannot be allowed to invest his wealth in even so secular an object as a clock-tower and so presume to status. A few years ago at least, it was not uncommon to read in the local newspapers that the Untouchables of such and such a village had been raided and beaten up precisely because their material condition had improved and they had let it be seen.

At the other end of the scale a Brahman does not need to support his status with wealth or the ostentation of it. The reader might think that we also have vestigial notions of decayed aristocracy, and of the mystique still attaching to blue blood. But however strong such notions may have been in the distant past, the cadet lines of our aristocratic families have, for the lack of financial support, merged with the commons and been lost to sight. In the Indian countryside, however, a Brahman is a Brahman by birth and is respected as such even if he is working, like one I knew, as a porter on a railway station.

There is a second qualification to the imitation of superior values which seems to have been stronger in the past, when the identity of caste was more marked in distinctive dress, style of turban and the like. To the extent that the members of a superior caste felt their identity in their clothes, they do not seem to have tolerated easily any imitation of these. People in a lower caste might win a grudging respect from their superiors if they abandoned meat-eating, but if they then started to wear their *dhoti*, for example, in the manner of a superior, then the reaction was often punitively savage.

I was told the following story as an instance from the good old days when men were men, and so on. There was a young Bareia of Sundarana who had got a little money together and took it into his head to grow the big curly moustache favoured by Patidar at that time; this was sixty years ago or so. In addition he sported the red turban. That, I am told, was the Patidar prerogative in those days. He then took a stroll through a Patidar village, smoking a little portable hookah such as any Patidar gentleman might smoke. Living in this village there was a powerful Patidar about whom a variety of ferocious stories were told. It seems that this character spotted the Bareia, had him seized by his retainers, summoned the village barber and ordered him to shave the upstart's face and, for good measure, his head as well. He then ordered the Bareia's hands and the offending hookah to be tied behind his back, and had him beaten round the village and out into the fields.

The fact that today one can rarely tell a man's caste from his appearance indicates that this particular aspect of caste identity has crumbled. This is not insignificant, for however trivial such matters might seem to us, the story I have told is typical as regards the amount of emotional investment there was in these external signs.

Finally, probably the greatest difference of all between imitation in Indian caste society and the Western aspiration to 'better oneself' or 'climb', is the underlying of morality. In our society we live according to a univocal scale of values. This does not mean, of course, that we all necessarily share the same values, but it does mean that we scale the values that we do have positively or negatively, we aspire to the good however we conceive it and eschew the bad, however we conceive that.

The Indian situation is more complex. We have to rid ourselves of the notion that 'low' in the caste hierarchy implies moral condemnation of such a kind that members of low castes ought to abandon their evil ways and conform to a universal set of values. Members of such castes are indeed said to be *halaki*, lightweight or shoddy, *nīch*, low and *kāli*, black—but in spite of being regarded as morally inferior, they are not morally condemned. One can very often hear the phrase *e lokone pāp nathi*, 'for those people it is not a sin', used in discussion of meat-eating, widow re-marriage, liquor drinking or any custom which the speaker regards as low. For this reason my own presence in Patidar houses was tolerated. It was known well enough that Europeans glut themselves on whisky and mutton; these two and biscuits were the commonest items of European diet that I heard mentioned. But for me the consumption of these things was not a sin as it would have been for one of them.[3] This relativity of a caste system is well known. There was, and probably still is, in Baroda a small group of professional men who followed a particular *guru*, said to be many centuries old. It was said of him that at one time he had been *guru* to a caste of thieves and had devoted himself to making them better thieves. This is the essence of traditional caste morality; whatever it is your lot to do, do it well.

Relativity counters any tendency to wholesale imitation of the superior. A family, or a section of a whole caste, must first have changed its image of itself before it would institute such changes. We can put it another way and say that the changes are not seen as innovations but as the recognition of an ideal which has been there all the time. Thus we read about castes that have 'changed' their status, but what is subjectively recorded is not a change, rather it is regarded as a reversion to a former status, said to have been lost to sight for generations. I am convinced that in the traditional caste system people do not aspire to higher status: they do not see their own society as a mobile one as we see our class society. They simply live the good life as they see it. What happens is, that for reasons we do not entirely understand, their notions of what constitutes the good life imperceptibly change.

The third ceremony that I attended on the night of the Great Eighth, over which a Brahman presided instead of a *bhuvo*, is an example of just such a change in one section of the Prabhudas Lakhujivalla lineage. I was also present on another occasion at a larger ceremony where a whole caste was involved in much the same process. The account of this ceremony brings this process more into the light and raises further items for our understanding.

The centre of activity is the shrine of Bhattiji, in Sundarana, the largest such that I saw in any village. Before describing the ceremony let me say more about this shrine and about Bhattiji himself.

The story of Bhattiji is, in various versions, well known

right across Gujarat. In essence it is as follows: Bhattiji was a Rajput by caste who was, like all of his caste, a devotee of the cow. While he was celebrating his wedding, and before he had completed the circumambulation of the fire which seals the contract, he received news that Muslims were attacking herdsmen and killing their cows. Bhattiji immediately left his bride by the sacrificial fire, took his sword and went to the defence of the cow. In the battle he was killed and so came to be revered as a martyr. I never heard any story which gave an account of his connexion with snakes and scorpions.

The shrine itself, *daheri*, is larger than usual, being over six feet in height and some five feet square, with the usual arched opening. On the back of the wall is the figure of a man in bas relief holding a small bow in his right hand and a short, broad dagger in his left. This is the dagger which, traditionally, the bridegroom carries on his marriage procession. Outside the shrine and to its left, set in the earth, is a large double trident—*trisul*. The central prong of the larger trident is itself made into a trident. Half way up the shaft of the *trisul* a small iron dish had been welded on to serve as a lamp. This *trisul* is the *shakti* of Bhattiji. I will return to this notion of *shakti* later.

The shrine is surrounded by a wall built recently but, for lack of money, not completed. The intention was to create a temple around the shrine, and this may yet be realized.

The major feast of Bhattiji is on the first day of the new year when a *mela*, fair (literally a concourse of people) is held. People come from surrounding villages, hawkers sell sweets, hot snacks, plastic toys and the like.

What we have here is a centre similar, though much smaller, to Ambājimātā's temple on Mount Abu. This shrine in Sundarana is locally regarded as the most powerful seat of Bhattiji. This seems to be a general pattern. Whether a god or goddess is recorded in the literary pantheon of India, or whether it is known only locally, it always seems to have a particular centre which is, so to speak, reflected in the minor centres, in villages and in houses throughout the territory. One may recognize such centres by the fact that on the day of the god or goddess the *mela* is held there. It seems that, in the past, these were much more comparable to the traditional European markets than they are today. I was told that formerly various village artisans would also bring their goods for sale and that, as in Europe, the fair was the great time for dealing in cattle. Today at the Bhattiji *mela*, for example, even the local artisans are not apparently concerned to take advantage of the commercial possibilities.

The central rite of the Bhattiji *mela* is the possession by Bhattiji of his *bhuvo* who, in a trance, shoots arrows representing those which Bhattiji himself fired at the Muslims. The fiction is that first, because he is normally an elderly man, he is suddenly endowed with such strength that he can shoot the bow, and secondly that, even though he shoots into the crowd, no one is ever hurt. At least when I witnessed the ritual, the bow was a light one well strung and the arrows themselves so light that they scarcely carried thirty-five yards. Secondly, the crowd opened up as soon as the arrows were set in the bow, leaving a wide avenue down which the *bhuvo* could shoot.

What is significant for this account is that Brahmans have only recently been introduced to the shrine of Bhattiji, certainly since 1940. Formerly the feeding of the god was performed by a Bareia *bhuvo* and his cook assistant. Today two offerings are made. The Bareia cooks sit outside the surrounding wall of the shrine and cook a kedgeree of mixed grains which one of them then takes in and offers to Bhattiji; thereafter the crowd fight for the remainder which is called *prasād*. This is traditional temple practice throughout India, the *prasād* is the remnant of the food which is supposed to have been eaten by the god, and the consumption of it carries considerable blessing. Today, while the Bareia cooks are performing their part, three Brahmans perform a fire sacrifice just inside the wall immediately before the archway of the

shrine. At the side of the shrine two Brahmans offer up the
coconuts and flowers which the faithful of all castes have
brought. They break the coconuts and return a half to the
donor as *prasād* and the other half is left within the shrine. At
a little distance three or four men sit quivering as the spirit
of the god possesses them. In the far corner the Rāval plays
on his drum.

This whole scene represents the new aspirations of the
Bareia in Sundarana, or at least those of an influential section
of the caste. The attempt to convert a relatively simple
shrine into a temple is itself significant. More striking is the
fact that Brahmans who, in this village, have hitherto kept
clear of Bhattiji worship, are now willing to officiate in front
of his shrine. The traditional priest or *bhuvo* has been
demoted and the food cooked by his associates, although
offered to the god, is cooked away from the main shrine. The
offerings of individuals are dignified and universalized by
being received and returned as *prasād* by Brahmans.

What do I mean by 'universalized'? Simply this: were the
offering to the god cooked by Bareia then it could not be
accepted as *prasād* by a member of any caste which regarded
itself as the superior of the Bareia. However much it may be
the leavings of a god who is respected by the Patidar, it is still
essentially food which has been cooked by a low caste from
which the Patidar would not normally accept food. On this
occasion I was particularly careful to see who took which
prasād. Some Patidar in fact ate the kedgeree *prasād* cooked
outside the wall by a Bareia. Other Patidar who came with
coconuts for the shrine ate the Brahman-offered coconut
prasād only. Of these, two young men were to my knowledge
cautioned by their mothers not to eat the inferior *prasād* of
grain. The behaviour on this occasion compares with that at
another sacrifice which I attended. On this occasion the
goddess was Meladimātā, the dirty goddess, to whom on
occasion people offer blood sacrifice. The Patidar who had
accepted the grain *prasād* of Bhattiji refused the grain

prasād of Meladimātā. Those who did eat it said that they were obliged to abstain from sexual intercourse that night on pain of suffering severe diarrhoea. Others said that there was no salt in the kedgeree, and for this reason the food could be eaten. I must add that I have never heard this particular reason adduced on any other occasion for eating food from an inferior caste.

The ceremony at the Bhattiji shrine perfectly represents an intermediary state between traditional low-caste and traditional high-caste behaviour, and the ambivalence of the situation is reflected in the behaviour of the Patidar in relation to the *prasād*. I naturally did not ask everybody what they had eaten and what they had not eaten, but I think it is significant that, on this occasion, Choto and his friends freely ate anything that they could lay their hands on while the young men of superior family, Surajben's closer kinsmen, were more diffident. One I do remember, who said that he took a little only out of respect for Bhattiji but could not eat more. This is surely a case of the individual salving his own conscience in a painfully ambiguous situation.

The reference to Meladimātā and the blood sacrifice reminds us of the second ceremony that I described earlier at which, it will be recalled, the *bhuvo* called at one point for a goat. The reference here was to a blood sacrifice which, today, most Patidar have eschewed entirely.

When I inquired into this matter it became clear to me that just as there are pure and impure castes so, but more absolutely, there are two categories of *mātā*—the clean and the unclean. There is, for example, in Sundarana, one nameless *mātā* whose shrine is out in the fields and who, it is said, refuses to enter any house, despite the prayers of her devotees, because she fears the pollution which might occur from the presence of women and strangers. She asks for and receives only vegetarian offerings. Other *mātā* ask for, and sometimes get, offerings of buffalo calf, goat and cock, and of these the archetypical *mātā* is Meladi. I was fortunately able to collect the story about this goddess which I give as near to the original manner as possible.

It is like this. Once all the gods were fighting with a *zan*, fearful and disgusting just like a member of the *Bhangi* caste, scavengers, or a *Vāghari*. They fought three long days and did not win. Indeed, they were so tired that the *zan* nearly conquered them. At night they sat down to consider the situation and one of them said 'Brothers, let's make a goddess from our faeces.' This they did. Their new goddess was so powerful that she fought the *zan* and killed him. Once she had achieved their purposes the gods ran off because they had made the goddess from filth. However, the goddess ran ahead and, by taking a short cut, out-distanced them and, by her magic, made a garden in the road along which they should pass. The gods came, saw the garden and sat down to drink from the well in the middle of it. As soon as they had drunk the water the goddess appeared to them and said 'Well, brothers, you have drunk my water and what are you going to do about that now?' They were in danger of becoming Untouchable and begged the goddess for mercy. She said 'Well, I will release you on condition that you give me a name and worship me.' After thinking about it they decided to call her Meladimātā because she was made from filth, *mel*. And that is how she has always been known.

The belief in Meladimātā, and other *mātā* of the same class, poses problems for the Western mind. Earlier writers on India tended to dismiss the continued existence of meat-eating gods in vegetarian populations, and of a non-Brahman priesthood, as survivals from a pre-Aryan age. The shortest way of dealing with this argument is to point out that something which has survived for three thousand years or more can scarcely be described as a waning fashion. More seriously, a basic premise of social anthropology is that all that goes on in society makes sense at some level or other, and that it will not do to dismiss, as a survival or a foreign importation, something which appears to contradict one's own expectations.

Let me give an instance, this time a hypothetical one, of a Brahman who had been bitten by a dog. If we imagine that, as a pure caste man and priest, he would have the same attitude towards Hadakaimātā and her *bhuvo* as a Christian priest might have towards the local palmist, we are much mistaken. Dog bites are the business of Hadakaimātā and her *bhuvo* is an Untouchable, that's all there is to it. If the Brahman wants protection he must have recourse to this *mātā* and he will do so as this is the obviously sensible thing to do. Dog bites are among the natural hazards of life. The situation is the same as regards the natural impurities which the Brahman and his family bring forth in the way of nature —blood, sweat and faeces; to deal with these exigencies of life the Brahman has recourse to the Barber, Washerman and Scavenger castes, with no sense of internal conflict.

Because Brahmans have only recently agreed to dignify the Bhattiji ritual by their participation, this does not mean that previously, if they were bitten by a snake or scorpion, they would not have gone to the shrine immediately to make an offering and to be cured. Thus the Patidar of Sundarana also regard all the *mātā* of their village as essential to their pantheon; they believe in them all. What kind of offering they make, whether or not they will eat the *prasād* or not, is another matter. I once asked Kishor, Surajben's husband, whether he was going to some festival in honour of a *mātā* and he said, in effect, 'Goodness no, I can't be bothered.' I said, 'Don't you believe in the *mātā*?' He looked at me as though I were mad and said, 'Of course I do, I just don't worship her, that's all.'

'Those who eat meat, offer it,' a Bareia said, trying to explain his theology to me. This is a simplification but it indicates that kind of sociological awareness that seems so common among Indian peasants. His remark indicates that

F

he is looking at *mātā* worship not only from the point of view of the recipient of that worship but also from the point of view of the worshippers. It is entirely true that there are some goddesses who demand meat only and some who insist upon vegetarian offerings only, but there are others, as for example Kalika, who receive whatever it is that their worshippers choose to offer them. However, if a Brahman is obliged to have recourse to a blood-eating *mātā*, and if that *mātā* demands a blood sacrifice, then she must have it. This does not mean that the Brahman will witness the sacrifice, let alone perform it or eat the *prasād* afterwards. He pays for the goat or whatever it might be. The rest is attended to by the *bhuvo*. Marked changes have taken place in the lifetime of the living, changes which are only pointed to when I say that, often enough today, people of vegetarian caste do not wish to be associated, however remotely, with the spilling of blood and give a pumpkin instead of an animal, or the model of a goat shaped from pounded pulse.

Let us briefly return to the second ceremony of the Great Eighth held by the descendants of Prabhudas Lakhuji. The *bhuvo* asked him for opium and was given a substitute; he, or rather the *mātā* in him, called for a goat and it was denied. Here we have a group of people at variance with their goddess and it is an interesting human situation. We have the traditionally ferocious Kālimātā ensconced as the reputed family goddess of a lineage, which, ostensibly at least, and for the majority I believe in practice, is now vegetarian. They are still sufficiently traditionally minded to call in the correct *bhuvo* of Kāli, a man of low caste, a meat eater and one who would offer meat to his own *mātā*. They must either convert the *bhuvo*, or abandon him just as their kinsmen who met later that evening had already done. At the third ceremony, it will be remembered, it was again Kalika who was being honoured.

I have another instance of the conversion of a goddess on an altogether grander scale, apparently involving the entire

Patidar caste. An account of this must start with a reference back to my earlier remark about *kuldevi* among the Patidar, and my suggestion that, when people claimed that a *mātā* who had been sitting in their house for several generations was a *kuldevi*, a lineage goddess, they were, for the sake of their own prestige, laying claim to an institution which is found among Brahmans and Rajputs (above, p. 54). It certainly seemed that in the past the desire to make this claim was stronger and, indeed, it may be that the ancient Patidar, like many low castes today, did indeed have one particular sacred place associated with a *mātā* to which they had a particular devotion. According to Brahmanic law it would be incorrect to call such a *mātā* a *kuldevi*: a *kuldevi* is one element of a whole complex, one of the components of a prestigious configuration which includes mythical ancestors, and an association with certain *veda*, which is only found in its full manifestation among Brahman and Rajput castes. We could put it more simply by saying that the *kuldevi* are the goddesses of distinct lineages within the caste, whereas the caste *mātā* is common to all lineages within the caste.

When I was first in Gujarat I made routine inquiries about the existence of *kuldevi* and caste *mātā*, and I was told that, indeed, the Patidar had a caste *mātā* which some Patidar informants referred to as a *kuldevi*. This was Ashapurimātā, a name which was translated to me as the wish-fulfilling *mātā*. I was told by a Patidar that they were obliged to go to her temple at least for the first hair-cutting ceremony of the eldest son, and that all Patidar would make a point of going to her temple at the annual *mela*.

Ashapurimātā had two main seats in Gujarat; one is near Bhuj in Kutch where she is the *kuldevi*, in the correct sense, of the Jadeja Rajputs. It is, I think, significant that the Jadeja Raputs were very influential in Gujarat in the nineteenth century; it is more than probable that the Patidar have imitated them in many particulars. The other seat of the *mātā* is at Navsāri in south Gujarat. This latter shrine does not appear to have any particular affiliation. Apart from these two main seats the shrine of Ashapurimātā, to which the Patidar refer when they speak of their '*kuldevi*' is a minor seat in the Kaira District.

I was determined to see this concourse of Patidar and made special arrangements, on a singularly hot day, to travel to Ashapuri. As a *mela*, the affair was not as disappointing as many *mela* often are. There was a reasonably large crowd, roundabouts, fortune-tellers and a wide variety of hawkers. However, I am reasonably confident that, apart from the few who accompanied me there, very few Patidar were present. Certainly I saw not one of those who had been most explicit in assuring me that, come what may, the Ashapurimātā *mela* was essential. The majority attendance was made up, as far as we could judge from the red head-scarves, of Bareia and the easily identifiable members of nomadic castes from Saurashtra.

I challenged some of my informants after I got home and they smoothly assured me that their remarks had referred to the past. Today, they said, it was too far to go for most people, who preferred, anyhow, to attend at Dākor or Vadtāl on holy occasions. In the expression of this preference the whole story is summed up: Dākor and Vadtāl are both centres of sectarian interest about which I shall have more to say later. Both from the spoken and the written word it seems likely enough that the Patidar were more assiduous in their attentions to Ashapurimātā in the past. Indeed, one would not have found the notion that they should attend her *mela* so widely expressed if there were not some truth in it. But today their interests have turned to other things.

The shrine itself bears witness to a considerable amount of attention in the past and indeed architecturally expresses the history of the development of this attention. The main shrine of the *mātā* is a poor affair, resembling a village shrine of the slightly better sort. It is somewhat larger than the village *daheri*, just about high enough for a man to stand upright inside. It was evidently old and in rather bad condition, unpainted and unrepaired on the outside. Inside, on the back wall were two figures in bas-relief, shaped like Egyptian mummies, their outlines crudely picked out in red paint. In answer to my inquiry I was told that there had originally been two sisters, Asha, the elder and the larger, and Puri. I have never heard this before and strongly suspect that it was the inventive creation of the moment.

In case that sounds arrogant, I should say that the villagers in Gujarat, at least, had a remarkable gift for etymologies. I remember Momad saying to me once that the origin of the word *dikaro*, a son, was from *dipa*, a lamp, and *karavun*, to make or do. The *dikaro*, therefore, is the one who offers the lamp to, presumably, the soul of his departed parents. There are no real grounds for such a derivation, and I have never heard anybody else offer it. Nor, indeed, was Momad proposing a serious etymology, rather he was using the language of etymology to make a poetic association, a sort of pun. I find many such 'etymologies' innocently recorded in my early notebooks.

To return to the shrine of Ashapurimātā, I would speculate that the unequal size of the two figures suggests an even more ancient history: it is usual when a couple is represented for the male to be the larger and for the female to be standing on his left. It is quite possible that the Ashapuri shrine was originally constructed for some quite other cult, now completely forgotten.

The contrast between this central, crude shrine and its surroundings is marked. There is a large compound wall surrounding it and, within this, the subsidiary shrines of the elephant-headed son of Shiva—Ganesha, the god of all auspicious beginnings and doorways, and Hanumān, the monkey god, the supporter of Rāmā in his battle with Rāvana, recounted in the Rāmāyana. Hanumān is a god cultivated by wrestlers and all who wish to achieve strength of body or mind through chastity. The most striking object in the whole compound is a large brass griffon couchant, its head facing the shrine. Between this and the shrine itself is an oval-shaped gap in the stone floor from which some brass inset has been removed. From the position and shape one can only assume that a tortoise figure, representing Vishnu in his *kurmāvatār*, was originally set into the stonework.⁴ The last substantial additions to the place were made by a wealthy Patidar of Petlad town, some time early in this century. Before the First World War he repaired the compound wall, built a *dharmsālā* and settled some land on a group of Brahmans who have, since that time, served the goddess. Since then, the Brahmans complain, they have received little in the way of substantial benefaction from anyone. The Brahmans to whom I spoke did not seem to be particularly aware of any special association between the shrine and the Patidar caste as a whole, but agreed that it was a good and holy place which people should visit, and where they could have their hair-cutting ceremonies performed.

The whole site of Ashapuri tells on the ground the same story as that of Bhattiji and the Bareia of Sundarana. Bhattiji is a god whose services are available to members of all castes, but the Bareia regard him as particularly their own. They themselves claim to be of Rajput origin and in the legend Bhattiji was a Rajput. The favourite name for him among the Bareia is Thakurji, respected lord, a title also used to address Rajputs. The Bareia have also surrounded his shrine with a wall with the intention, currently abandoned, of covering it to create a large temple. Without the resources of the wealthy Patidar they have been unable to decorate it as finely as the shrine of Ashapurimātā, but they have persuaded Brahman to officiate and, at least today, there is no hint that blood sacrifice is offered to Bhattiji.

It is very difficult for a Bareia to come up in his world. The caste is by and large poor and, where the Patidar reign, landless. There are, however, a few villages in which the Bareia are the majority landowners, and two families of Bareia in

Sundarana, who had affinal relations with such landowning Bareia, regarded themselves as spokesmen for their caste, and were actively engaged in reformist activities directed against smoking, drinking and loose behaviour generally. Their houses, although in no way materially superior to those of others, were decidedly cleaner and more orderly. They bathed more frequently and thoroughly than others and even walked and talked with what I can only describe as a methodical reserve, quite noticeable when they were among their more loose-limbed, gesticulating and vociferous caste fellows. One of them had accompanied me to Ashapurimātā but, in common with his immediate kinsmen, his chosen place of worship was Dākor. I mention this because if attendance at Dākor, or some other sectarian centre, comes to be part of the expected behaviour of the respectable Bareia, then Bhattiji's shrine may go the same way as that of Ashapurimātā, as the Bareia like the Patidar turn to other forms of worship.

The very signs with which the shrine of Ashapurimātā is surrounded indicate the lines along which the Patidar of an earlier generation endeavoured to make their goddess respectable. Shiva and Vishnu are, it is well known, together with Brahma, worshipped throughout India in one form or another, and their worship is supported by an ancient and rich literary tradition. The figures of Ganesha and Hanumān represent the two great gods Shiva, and Vishnu as Rama; their presence outside the shrine of Ashapurimātā equates her with their cult. The location of the griffon outside the shrine equates it with a temple devoted to Shiva. In this part of Gujarat a small Shiva temple will be found in every village, and outside facing it is the representation of the bull *nandi*, his vehicle. I never saw anywhere else the vehicle, in this case a griffon, of a *mātā* so represented outside her shrine. The surviving evidence that Vishnu, in his tortoise form, had been placed between the griffon and the temple, confirms my impression that the shrine was in process of being equated to the superior cult. Vishnu is often represented in this form and situation outside Shiva temples although contradictory reasons for the association are given. Some who would account themselves exclusive worshippers of Shiva say that it represents the subordination of Vishnu to their God. Others, perhaps more ecumenically minded, say that the figure is introduced to remind the faithful that both Vishnu and Shiva are parts of, or manifestations of, the same undivided godhead.

These changes in the worshipping habits of individuals, families, descent groups and whole castes, are symptomatic of changes that have taken place throughout central Gujarat within living memory. Like most people who know India only through her sacred literature, I supposed when I first arrived that vegetarian and non-vegetarian cults were entirely exclusive the one of the other. I think also that I tended to impute a moralistic attitude to vegetarians as regards their non-vegetarian countrymen. I will offer evidence later to suggest that, in fact, today such exclusive and moralistic attitudes are beginning to develop; but there is no doubt that, both in the remote and recent past, the two cults were interdependent, as in some parts of Gujarat they still are.

In the mid-1960s a Brahman in Saurashtra, the western section of Gujarat, described to me the house and village foundation sacrifices in which he was a specialist. He described to me how a pit was dug at the chosen site and how a priest would sacrifice a goat or buffalo calf in such a manner that its head and blood poured into the pit. I asked if the priest were a Brahman. 'No,' he said, 'How could a Brahman do that? It is a priest of the caste for whom I am doing the work.' 'Does he do it in your presence?' I asked. 'No, I come along afterwards,' he said. 'I perform my sacrifice on top of the beast's head.' This was the kind of talk that I had never heard from a Brahman in Central Gujarat, among the Patidar, and I pressed him on the matter of blood sacrifice, asking him whether this was not *hinsa*, violence and therefore bad. 'Of course it's *hinsa*,' he said. 'So what? You can't have a founda-tion ceremony without a blood sacrifice, it's essential and that's that.'[5]

In Sundarana, back in the 1950s the villagers had success-fully concealed the fact of blood sacrifice from my eyes. The practice was by that time rare, but it still occurred. Initially they denied that it occurred at all and it was a pure chance that I came across evidence of its practice. I was walking in the village with no particular purpose in mind, and noticed a handsome young black goat tethered by the side of a hut. The houseowner was sitting outside and, for the sake of making conversation I complimented him on the goat's sleek appearance. 'Ah yes,' he said, 'he's a three-day guest.' This is an idiom used of honoured guests. The generosity of even the poorest Indian peasant is astonishing but not foolish, and there are many proverbs and jokes about guests who overstay their welcome, three days being the conventional period. The goat was an honoured guest because he had been dedicated to a *mātā* and was due to be sacrificed shortly. I could scarcely ask Kishor, at that time my immediate host in the village, to keep me informed about the time of the sacrifice as he had been most strenuous in assuring me that such things did not occur. I hinted to a young Bareia that were such an event to take place I would not be uninterested in witnessing it. I said that I had seen the goat and understood that there was some possibility of a blood sacrifice. He said, rather guardedly, that he would see to it that I was kept informed, but after that I am not quite sure what happened. Placed as I was in Kishor's circle it seemed indelicate to inquire into a matter which was clearly distasteful to them, and one which, moreover, they clearly wished to conceal from me. When I pressed the young Bareia he told me that the sacrifice had been delayed because there had been a death in the family, and that now it was impossible to give a certain date in the foreseeable future. The goat vanished from its tethering peg, and all my inquiries were met by a smiling and apparently helpful evasiveness. A few weeks later I had to leave Sundarana for a few days and was told on my return that, most unfortunately, the auspicious time for the sacrifice had occurred while I was away.

About the past the villagers were less reticent. Kishor himself was reminiscing one evening to a crowd of us younger men about the bad old days, and he seemed to me to be thoroughly enjoying his recollections. There had just been a *mela* at the largest Shiva temple in the village, situated about half a mile away, across the railway line, the site, some said, of the original Sundarana village. I had said that it had seemed a pretty poor affair. In the course of the day scarcely two hundred people had attended and of these remarkably few were from Sundarana itself. There had been one hawker rather half-heartedly selling small plastic toys, and an enterprising Bareia family had set up a small stall to sell *bhajian*, fritters, and *sev*, a kind of dried and spiced spaghetti. A few people had made offerings of coconuts at the temple itself, but there was no special *puja*; the priests, whom I shall describe later, had deserted the temple.

Kishor spoke of the *mela* of the old days, of the hundreds of people who had come and of the market at which artisans from Sundarana and other villages sold their manufactures. It had, he said, been a great day for dealing in cattle, bullocks, buffalo and goats. 'Was there a special *puja*?' I asked. 'Oh God, yes,' he said, 'all that night there was a big do, all the *bhuvo* of the village would be there trembling away, great carryings on.' The word he used here was *tophān*, naughtiness, but the word was used with such relish that I think I am right to translate it as I have. 'What do you mean by carryings on?' I said. 'Sacrifice,' he replied. 'Goats, buffalo, calves, anything and everything, lots of them.' He chatted on about the drinking and the girls, the practical jokes and the drunken brawls, and, when he had quite finished, concluded, very properly, 'However, that was all fifty years ago. We're all civilized now.'

The verb he used here is worth a note; *sudhāravuṅ*, to grow better, to be reformed, to improve, to be enlightened, to be civilized. The same verb is used of families or castes who, although lower than the speaker, are given a certain grudging respect because, like the Bareia families that I mentioned, they make some effort towards respectability. The use of the word in this way implies a recognition of a dynamic in caste society which is nevertheless denied by the ideology of caste.

There seems to be a hiatus in the collective thinking on this matter of which I could cite other examples. Briefly, while Kishor could give instances of what is now considered to be low-caste behaviour among Patidar of the preceding generations, he would not draw the conclusion that at that time the general estimation of the Patidar was lower than it is today. Equally, he could say, rather patronizingly, of a small group of Bareia that they were reformed, in that they were vegetarian, respectably dressed and in general measured up to his own standards of good behaviour, without for all that admitting what the cumulative effect of such changes must be.

I will give one more example of this conflict between a static and a dynamic view in this society. The Patidar of Sundarana do not rank very high in the caste overall. It is probably that they were late in shaking off the Rajput ascendancy which at least some of their wealthier caste fellows in other villages had dispensed with early in the nineteenth century. Whatever may be the historic fact, the Bareia of Sundarana claim that originally they were the landowners and that the Patidar worked in their fields. They expressed this claim by saying that they once 'sent food to the Patidar'. Now, as in the past, if a man employs field labour part of the payment will be food cooked in his own kitchen and sent out to the fields. If the members of one caste eat the food of another they are usually the inferiors and at best the equals of that caste. The Bareia are, then, claiming not merely a politico-economic superiority in the past but, most probably, a superior status in the caste hierarchy. Today no Patidar would wish it to be known that he had eaten food prepared in a Bareia kitchen. Nevertheless the Patidar of Sundarana admit that part of the Bareia claim which relates to land ownership. When I asked them about the food side of it they said that this was partly true, but that the food had been *pakka*, that is prepared with *ghi* or milk, not *kachcha*, prepared with water only or oil. *Pakka* foods are regarded, in certain contexts, as pure foods which can be exchanged between castes. They are certainly not as subject to pollution as food prepared in water. They are, however, expensive, certainly not everyday foods. The idea of a landlord sending out such meals to his field labourers is really absurd, but this is the only way in which my Patidar informants could reconcile the absolute of caste status with the relativities of historical change.

Evidence of a recent inter-dependence of the pure and impure, vegetarian and bloody cults, comes not only from the Patidar. I came across it also in a Bania family. Most Patidar would admit that the Bania have superior status to themselves, and, in the family with which I stayed, the standards of caste orthodoxy were very high and closely observed. I was nevertheless told that the head of the house, at this time a very old man, regarded a visit to the temple of Ambajimātā as an essential part of his annual devotions. In his youth he had witnessed blood sacrifices there and not only this, he had also received the *tilak*, mark on the brow, from the blood of the sacrificial beast and brought a blood-stained handkerchief home with him as a blessing for his family. In this case the picture is not confused by a history of caste mobility as it tends to be for the Patidar. In the past the Patidar may well have been the active participants in the inferior cult in which they now participate only passively if at all. The Bania, on the other hand, whatever other reputation they may have, are, and throughout the recorded history of Gujarat have always been, a byword for the observance of high-caste and vegetarian practice. Many sections of the Bania caste are also Jains who carry the avoidance of violence to living creatures to extremes. For this Bania in his youth the violent cult was as necessary a part of his world as the non-violent. The best contrast that I can think of is that of a man in our own society who might feel guilty about eating meat because he had not, as he might put it, the courage to kill the chicken or the bullock that he liked to eat. For such a mind which tends to totalize the universe and at the same time individualize the consciousness of it, the more thoroughgoing relativity of the traditional Indian world view must seem strange.

I conclude this chapter with a quotation from a popular text devoted to the cult of the *mātā*: its title may be rendered in English as *The Most Glorious History of the Goddess.*[6] This is a thick book, cheaply bound with rather garish illustrations, printed in large characters for easy reading. In similar format the great classics of Indian literature, the Purānas, the Rāmāyana, the Mahābhārata, become available to the villagers at a remarkably low price. These works contain not only the stories of the gods but also a great deal of moral exhortation and prescriptions for the performance of rituals. In the book from which I quote there is, as so often, a dialogue between two characters, in this case a Brahman and a king. The discussion relates to the appropriate ceremonies for the Nine Nights and I translate the king's question in full because it is typical of the style:

The king asked: 'Oh most high Brahman, when the Nine Nights come then in what manner are the holy rites to be performed, when the autumn festival of the Nine Nights comes what specially must be done at that time, that tell me? Oh thou endowed, with the highest wisdom, most excellent Brahman, what fruits may we expect from the

Nine Nights and what rites should we perform then, be magnanimous and amply explain.'

The Brahman then holds forth about the Nine Nights, the reason why they occur at that time of the year, the preparation and ablutions which must be performed, the way in which the tabernacles for the *mātā* are to be prepared, and so on. After listing various offerings he continues:

Those who are flesh eaters must kill animals and among these the buffalo calf, the goat and the boar are regarded as the highest offerings. Those beasts which have been slaughtered in front of the *mātā* go to the eternal heaven, therefore, O sinless king, this result of the goddess worship frees the killers from the sin of animal murder. Throughout the sacred literature there is talk of violent and nonviolent sacrifices and it is most certain that animals that have been offered to the gods rest without any question in heaven.

The Brahman then goes on to speak of the construction of sacrificial pits. The anonymous modern editor of this text has footnoted the passage that I have quoted at two points. On the subject of meat eaters offering sacrifice he comments:

Although many Brahmans are meat eaters they should not openly make flesh offerings. This prohibition derives from the first part of the Kalikapurana. That we are to understand that this custom is directed to Kshatriya appears from that section called Sharadatilak which says [here follow two lines of Sanskrit which the editor glosses in Gujarat] Pure Brahman who follow the ordinances should make pure (*sātvik*) offerings for, when they have abandoned offerings associated with violence, these then become for other castes the highest.

The editor/translator goes on to cite from the Purana other confirmatory texts and concludes with one indicating that only *mātā* or goddesses can receive blood sacrifice. He asks the reason for this and quotes again a passage which he glosses as follows:

The goddess is accounted the presiding genius of divine knowledge and as the termination of a life span is inherent to that knowledge for this reason this offering to the goddess is reckoned to be the most dear.

The second annotation relates to that part of the original quotation which absolves the slayers from guilt. The annotator comments:

'This passage must also be regarded as directed towards the Kshatriya and not to the Brahmans. It is possible that there might be in the Kshatriya mind some worry about this violence and this is said for their comfort. In point of fact any man of any caste can offer any god or goddess a pure offering, indeed this is the better. Anyone who kills an animal for a ritual is re-born in a violent or passionate form unless he is able to purify his intentions, this must be taken as axiomatic.'

NOTES

1. In modern India four major calendars prevail: the Hindu, the Muslim, the Zoroastrian and the Christian/western secular. In the village the western secular calendar co-ordinates the business activities and those having to do with government, education etc. Marriages, rituals, fasts and festivals are governed by the Hindu lunar calendar according to which each month is divided into a dark, inauspicious, and a bright, auspicious half. The day of the full moon, *punam*, is the holiest day of the month most suitable for temple visits.
2. For an example of this, see Adrian C. Mayer, *Caste and Kinship in Central India*, London, 1960, Chapter 4.
3. Needless to say I did not eat meat in the village; that would have taxed the tolerance of this morality too far. Similarly, although according to the theory I was classified as untouchable, I was not so treated so long as I did not associate with the Untouchables.

4. There are three kinds of divine incarnation, *amsha*, *āvesha* and *avatāra* of which the last is the only complete incarnation; the others are partial or temporary. It is believed that Vishnu becomes incarnate at moments or periods of human or cosmic crisis: the tortoise incarnation is the second of ten which are particularly venerated; in this form Vishnu supported on his back the Mandara mountain which gods and demons used as a churning pole to raise out of the ocean certain precious objects and qualities.

5. The misunderstanding between myself and the Brahman exemplifies a change in the significance of *hinsa*. For him the word preserved its neutral meaning, killing; for me the term had Vaishnavite and Gandhian connotations of evil.

6. *Shrimad Bhagavati Bhāgavat*, published by the Krishna Book Stall, Sharāf Bazaar, Bhāvnagar, price Rs. 6/-. The subsequent quotations are taken from Chapter 2, section 27.

4

The Old Pattern—Purity with Impurity

The annotator's comments reflect an embarrassment in the face of his text very different from that of my Saurashtrian Brahman, for whom the inter-dependence of non-violence and violence, vegetarian and blood sacrifice constituted no problem. In this chapter I show how the embarrassment is shared and exemplified in modern and changing circumstances. The tendency, especially in this part of Gujarat, is towards a resolution of the 'problem' in favour of an unequivocal vegetarianism. How this develops and what its implications are, I hope to show in a later chapter. First, however, I must try to reconstruct a picture of the past in the light of which both the present 'problem' and the tendencies to the future may be better understood.

I was talking to my old Bareia friend, one day, about the *mātā*. He, rather more than most people in the village, had been to several places of pilgrimage and was generally more knowledgeable about these matters than anyone else. He said in the hearing of others that all the *mātā* were one, and that one was the *shakti*, power, energy, of God. Interestingly enough the people around him laughed at this. In fact, there is good evidence to suppose that what we now see in Gujarat of the worship of *mātā* are the fragments, so to speak, of a much older pattern of worship. I hasten to add that they are not mere survivals of an older form of worship; clearly they have their place in the present-day village, people make use of them as beings whose existence both explains the source of disease or misfortune and provides the cure. What I do affirm is, however, that the traditional pattern which related the *mātā* to each other and linked them with Shiva has largely disappeared. The complex of belief and worship directed towards Shiva and the *mātā* jointly is known as *shaktipuja.*

Although the majority of people in Sundarana and in surrounding villages would, if asked, profess themselves to be Vaishnavites, followers of the Lord Vishnu, the commonest sacred sites in this part of Gujarat, apart from the fanes and shrines of the *mātā*, are the temples of Shiva. In Sundarana, as in almost all of the smaller villages which I visited, there was no proper temple dedicated to Vishnu in any of his forms. In Sundarana itself in fact there was one Patidar who had a particular devotion to Rama and to his consort Sita; he had given over a room in his house to their images. There every evening he performed an elaborate *puja* to which the public was invited. Apart from this there was nothing. Sundarana is quite typical in this respect: it has four Shiva temples of which only one is in the residential area of the village. The other three are within convenient walking distance.

In this part of Gujarat Shiva is known universally as Mahādev, Great God. His temples are invariably dedicated to him as lord of some moral or material good, Siddeshwar, lord of supernatural power, Jareshwar, lord of wealth. The essential object in his temple is his phallic representation, the *ling*, or *lingam*. This is a cylinder of stone rounded at the top which is set into a *yoni*, a simple circle with a rim around it opening at one point into a long grooved duct which acts as a sluice for the water and liquid offerings which are poured upon the *ling*. Above the *ling*, hanging from the dome of the temple, there is usually an unglazed earthenware pot hanging in such a way that it drips perpetually on to the *ling*. To one side of the chamber, in line with the duct leading from the *yoni*, is a drain hole at the base of the side wall. In drought years when the monsoon is weak, or fails, this drain hole can be plugged up and the whole chamber flooded so that the *ling* is entirely immersed in water.

Behind the *ling* and higher up the wall a niche contains a small figure of Shiva's consort, Pārvati, which is swathed to the eyes in cloth. Outside the door of the inner chamber there will usually be figures of Hanuman and Ganesha on the observer's left and right respectively.

In only one such temple did I see the bird figure of *garud*, the vehicle of Vishnu. The villagers were less perturbed by the anomaly than I was and said that they presumed that the *achārya*, the priest or teacher, who had ordered the building of the temple must have had some good reason for it. The main chamber of every Shiva temple is fronted with a small, covered forecourt open on three sides and usually accessible by steps. This forecourt is covered by a dome smaller than that surmounting the main chamber; in it there hangs a large bell which the worshipper strikes as he enters the temple. Inside this forecourt or usually outside and facing the *ling* is a stone figure of the bull *nandi*, the vehicle of Shiva. It is not uncommon to find also a representation of Vishnu in his tortoise incarnation, on the ground between the *nandi* and the *ling*.

The typical village temple is not a large affair. It is about twenty feet long and seldom more than twelve feet wide. It invariably faces to the east.[11]

Sundarana's most important Mahādev temple is the one at which the disappointing *mela* occurred (above, p. 74). The main temple is associated with two smaller temples of more recent construction and all three are surrounded by a stone wall with a ruined cloister intended to serve as a *dharamsālā* for pilgrims. The wall and cloister are said to have been built by a wealthy Bania of the village of Rās (some five miles away). The tradition is that in the past the Bania of that village used to bring their sons here to have their first hair-cuts. From what is left of the *dharamsālā* wall it looks as though, in the past, it may also have served some defensive purpose, for the walls are thick and parapets run along the top. The major temple is known as Jareshwar. The *ling* is believed to have been discovered hundreds of years ago by a Rabari, a member of the nomadic herdsmen caste which travels across central Gujarat once a year in search of pasture. It seems that he used to tie his cattle to a certain tree at night and discovered when he came to milk them in the morning that they were dry. He resolved to keep watch one night to see who was stealing his milk and saw the cows discharging their milk voluntarily into the ground on a certain spot under the tree. He dug there and discovered the *ling*. On this account villagers sometimes represent the name as *jhādeshwar*, the lord of the tree.

The smaller and more recent temples owe their existence to the presence near this temple for many years of a band of Gosain sadhus. The Gosain are a somewhat mysterious people particularly associated with the worship of Shiva. Some of them are married, some, at least temporarily, take to the nominally celibate life of the sadhu and wander from temple to temple or, as at Sundarana, settle to make a permanent *āshram*. A truly holy sadhu is not said to die as other men die, rather he goes into his final trance, his *mahāsamādhi*, and is buried sitting cross-legged at the bottom of a shaft facing to the north. The shaft is sealed with a small square structure surmounted usually by a squat four-faceted dome. This structure itself comes to be known as the *samādhi* of so and so. There are several such *samādhi* by the Mahādev temples at Sundarana and over one of them a *daheri* has been erected. This is said to be the *samādhi* of some famous leader of the group and his footprints are represented in marble on the floor of the shrine.

In other villages in Gujarat I have seen Mahādev temples at which Gosain ascetics still perform a daily worship. When

I first visited Sundarana there was a Gosian couple with their children living up at the Jareshwar Mahādev compound. They had no permanent habitation there and had fixed up a simple shelter against the walls of the ruined *dharmsālā*. I assume that had there been sufficient offerings, or had they perhaps found a wealthy patron in Sundarana, they would have settled as others have done in other villages; but after a few months they packed up and went without any leave-taking.

The Gosain are particularly associated with Shiva and claim to be his peculiar priests. They are not Brahmans but their claim is admitted by Brahmans. While they were in residence at Jareshwar they adopted the Mahādev temples, kept them clean and made small offerings at morning and night. Villagers, who would otherwise walk boldly into the inner chamber to lay flowers or pour water on the *ling*, gave their offerings to the Gosain to take them in, as though his presence did indeed dignify the offering a little. Some families cling to an old practice of not lighting the house lamp until the evening offering, signalled by the bell, had been made at Jareshwar. When no regular offering was made after the Gosain had left, no one seemed much put out however. For a brief period, when the monsoon seemed unduly delayed, a group of about six old men made a regular practice of going up to Jareshwar in the evening to sing a *bhajan*, hymn, and light a lamp for Mahādev, but once the monsoon had broken the cult was not sustained.

There is another caste in this part of Gujarat associated with Shiva, Mahādev, and that is the Tapodhan Brahmans. Although they are regarded as inferior by other Brahman their right to worship Mahādev is admitted by all. A peculiarity which these two castes share, in addition, is that both are permitted by custom to eat the *sivnirmālya*, the offerings (literally, the abandoned flowers) of Shiva. This is the one god whose offerings are not normally consumed by the faithful as *prasād*. The word *sivnirmālya* in fact is now a byword for any worthless, expendable thing. It is not for nothing that on the very few occasions that a sacrifice is offered at Jareshwar Mahādev in Sundarana today, it is a sacrifice of the pumpkin which is explicitly substituted for an animal. If Kishor's reminiscences of what had gone on in his youth are correct, then we have more than a hint here that part of the offering was flesh which, in that context, was the perquisite of the attendant priest. Perhaps this is one reason for the degraded position of the priests of Shiva. But here I anticipate a later argument.

Nowadays, Sundarana with its priestless, cultless Mahādev temples is typical of villages throughout this part of Gujarat. The temples are convenient landmarks for arranging meetings. Because they are usually surrounded by trees they are cool places to walk to in the evening for a chat and a smoke. Sometimes people may show evidence of a minor devotion in that, before they sit down, they will first slip off their sandals and go into the shrine. bow to the *ling* with folded hands and say 'Jay Mahādev', glory and power to Mahādev, but they rarely leave an offering. I saw no man in Sundarana who regularly wore the three horizontal yellow stripes on his brow that mark the devotee of Shiva. Certainly, the villagers were not much given to wearing such marks in general, but such as did wore some mark signifying dedication to Vishnu.

Shiva's night, Shivrātri, which falls on Kāli Chaudas, the Black Fourteenth, is also the eve of the Feast of Lights, Divāli, and tends to be lost in the hectic preparations for the latter festival, which ushers in the new lunar year.

I have described a decaying, if not totally decayed, cult. The remnants, the temples, the *mātā*, the odd beliefs survive, each one integrated with the day-to-day life of the villagers in Sundarana. It is nevertheless necessary to try to understand what this cult amounted to in its heyday. Social anthropologists are much averse, and quite rightly, to reconstructing the past from fragments, but I shall, nevertheless, make the attempt because we are not talking simply about changes in beliefs, as though beliefs could exist in some kind of vacuum. Older beliefs about Shiva and the *mātā* have changed as beliefs about caste and human relations have also changed. I shall discuss later the direction in which modern changes are turning, but we shall be able to appreciate them the better if we have a rather more precise notion of the state of affairs which existed before the time that I am describing.

Shakti means essentially capacity to do, power; in a theological context this is the power of the divine. Throughout India this power is symbolized as feminine. Beyond this point we cannot generalize because a host of different theologies and cults centre upon the divine femininity, with a variety of emphases. We could make a very general tripartite division in India accordingly as people regard Shiva, Vishnu and Shakti respectively as the supreme being. Such a distinction is not very satisfactory and has less validity even than the distinction between Catholic and Protestant in our own civilization. Not only does worship of any one include worship of the other two, but also there is no real uniformity or continuity between the different cults as they have emerged historically, or are found today in any one area. *Shaktipuja* in Gujarat is not the same thing as *shaktipuja* in Bengal, for instance; there, one has the impression, the Divine Mother is worshipped by some as the fullest manifestation of divinity superior to male gods.

In order to understand *shaktipuja* in Gujarat we have to understand also a distinction in Indian thought which corresponds to our own distinction in theology between the transcendent and the immanent forms of the divine. The divine can be regarded as *saguna* or *nirguna*, having attribues or not having attributes. As *saguna* the divine has a person and can be thought of as male or female, as *nirguna* the divine is simply 'It' or 'That'. Just as amongst ourselves the distinction between the transcendent and the immanent god is not exclusive, but rather complementary in that both are 'true' and the verification of one does not demand the falsification of the other, so the Indian Divine is at once *saguna* and *nirguna*. The distinction gives us an opening into Gujarat *shaktipuja*, for the word *shakti* refers to the immanent, manifest and acknowledged energy or power of the divine in the world. Because it is in the world it participates in the *māya*, play illusion, of the world, and is therefore characterized as inferior together with the world of forms and appearances in which it is manifest; for this reason it is characterized in Indian thought as feminine. In relation to this *shakti*, Shiva is the transcendent Lord, superior and masculine. Clearly he is also *saguna*, manifest in his *ling* in temple after temple, his legend and rites are prescribed in the Shivpurana, but by the same token he is also *nirguna* as the supreme being, transcendent, unknowable, unqualified and formless.

In the Indian pantheon there is no god whose co-present masculinity and femininity is more explicit in his manifest form than Shiva. The *ling* rests invariably in the vulvic *yoni* It may be wondered whether the villagers are aware of this sexual aspect, and the answer seems to be that some are and some are not. A friend of mine in Baroda, an anthropologist, told me that his aunt was quite shocked when he made her understand what the *ling* was. On the other hand some village women, of somewhat lower social pretension than Surajben certainly, were capable of making jokes based on a greedy appreciation of the phallic symbolism. Whatever doubts there may be on this score I can certainly affirm that today in Sundarana even a rudimentary knowledge of the theology that I have sketched out is almost entirely lacking, as witness the derision which met the old pilgrim's pronouncement that the *mātā* was the *shakti*, power, of God. It will be remembered that the double trident stuck in the ground outside Bhattiji's shrine was referred to by some as Bhattiji's *shakti*, although no one could say why (above, p. 60).

When I was describing Jareshwar Mahādev at Sundarana, I said that it had, as most such temples do, a niche in the back wall for a little image of his consort, Pārvati. Apart from the recognition of the connexion the villagers address no special cult to Pārvati; there is no other *daheri* dedicated to her, and she is not referred to as Pārvatimātā with the other *mātā* of the village. Nevertheless, Pārvati is the essential link between Mahādev and the *mātā*.

In Gujarat literature, Pārvati has two aspects, each represented by various forms. In her peaceful aspect she is Gauri, Himavati, Jagan and Bhavāni; in her fierce forms she is Durga, Kāli, Shyāma, Chandi and Bheirāvi. It is in her fierce form that she can be placated with blood sacrifice. There are many other names and some, like Durga in Bengal, and Kāli (as Kālikā) and Ambajimātā, or Ambika, have autonomous cults centred on them with their own myths and legends. This only develops a capacity of the entire complex to contain fragmentation and individualization of its elements. Every *mātā* has some legend behind her which accounts for her name, her habits and, sometimes, for her particular manifestations at one spot rather than at another. At the same time every *mātā* can be equated with any other, all can be reduced to one, and that one in turn merged into the ineffable.

The same pattern underlies the representation of Shiva, Mahādev. For the Shivaite, the Lord Shiva is the ultimate source of being, of whom all other gods are only the appearances. No villager would be so stupid as to make separate identifications for Shiva in Sundarana and, shall we say, Shiva in the nearby village of Gorel. Nevertheless each Shiva *ling* is qualified, as I said earlier, by a particular name and the reason for the location of it on that particular spot is accounted for by a particular history. The *mātā* in each village may be peculiar to that village or they may be duplicated elsewhere, but all can be equated with the Pārvati of Shiva in that village who is, with

Shiva himself, local and particular as well as unlocalized and general.

As Shiva is to his *shakti* so the *adisakti*, original *shakti* or Pārvati, is to the *mātā*.

All this should not be so strange to the European reader who knows something of Catholic Christianity in practice. Modern fieldwork in Spain and in Italy enables us to see how the Virgin Mary is one and, at the same time, many in her local manifestations, and how the local manifestation becomes, on occasion, for the peasants an identification. Thus we hear that the Virgin of this village is more powerful than the Virgin of another village. The Virgin as Queen of the Saints is associated with a host of saints, some of which are found elsewhere while others are of purely local derivation, some indeed have not even been elevated to the altars of the Church.

I give this parallel only to assist understanding because, despite a superficial resemblance, these two structures are very different in their significance, just as the social organizations to which we relate them are obviously different. The most striking difference in content is of course the co-presence of the pure and the impure, the peaceable and violent forms of *shakti*, which reflect the co-presence in traditional caste society of pure and impure castes, interdependent upon one another to run life in the traditional Indian way.

A lot has been written about a process which M. N. Srinivas many years ago called *sanskritization*, an unhappy term, which he used to describe the way in which inferior castes imitate superior castes. In his early work he rather gave the impression that this was an unqualified process. He spoke as though there were somewhere, in some established canon of Sanskrit literature, a defined source of beliefs which, by various media and through the attempts of castes to 'better themselves', gently filtered their way down to the masses. Such a process could only have for its end result the homogenization of the entire population in matters of belief, which is palpably not the case.[2]

What we have just seen is that so long as the caste system maintained its traditional structure of belief, there had always to be a distinction between high and low, pure and impure. One *mātā* might be pure for this caste and impure for that; a custom or practice that is today the mark of a high caste can tomorrow become the distinctive trait of a low caste; but always the elements, from whatever source they may derive, are subordinate to the pattern in which the structure of caste arranges them.

I should say something finally about the notion of a 'true source' which implies an accepted canon or centre of orthodoxy. The comparison between Western and Indian society brings out similarities as well as important differences. The reader has only to think of the English language which, despite considerable homogenization, exists in various dialects. He will perhaps be initially disposed to say, 'Yes, but these are different dialects of correct English.' But his notion of correct English derives from a centre which he and those around him have selected for reasons which do not inhere in the nature of language. Is the centre of correct English the same for the inhabitant of Edinburgh as it is for the inhabitant of Ohio? As Collingwood, discussing Vico, says of Italian, 'language is what the people who use it think it is'.[3]

But obviously the Western world does have its centres of orthodoxy. We might even say that the Western world loves the notion of the one true version and this is particularly so of its sacred texts. But what is the Bible but the product of a series of decisions made at different times by different bishops and communions about the validity of different texts? With a growing tendency to centralization the selective process has come to a halt, but today the Catholic version still contains books which are omitted from the Protestant version, and we have yet to see what will come of the famous Dead Sea Scrolls. More generally Christianity itself can only be said to exist in the millions of individuals in which it is in any way manifest, who profess and call themselves Christians. What they share is not a common body of beliefs and practices so much as a notion that there *is* one true communion, sect or Church which is usually the one of the individual speaking.

The Indian tradition is less preoccupied with centrality and a desire for the exclusive and the essential. The great texts which lay down social laws, expound philosophies and moralities, prescribe rituals and worship, as texts existed in their multiplicity. Their unity was nominal. Just as every local ling is *the* ling of Shiva, so the Mahābhārata existed in the multiplicity of its versions, each of which related the great names to particular local beliefs and legends, and set the scene in local, familiar surroundings.

The body of Indian Sanskrit scholars, in this matter inspired by Western ideals, collates and compares; the idea that there should be a one true text is rapidly receiving an embodiment in the creation of one. But this received version must inevitably dispense with, as corrupt, the localizations in which the Mahābhārata historically had its existence. The effect would be rather as though some synod in the New Delhi were to decide on the qualification, pedigree and precise duties of a Brahman, and permit henceforth only licensed and trained Brahmans to practise. Historically all that Brahmans have in common is a belief in the idea of Brahmanhood and of its superiority; to be a Brahman is to be among the purest castes in any area. But how that superiority and purity manifest themselves and are realized in any particular Brahman or group of Brahmans depends upon the particular circumstances of the time.

I have laboured this point together with a brief account of the *shaktipuja* complex which now lies in ruins, because the changes at work in the villages can only be appreciated for their revolutionary qualities if we have some understanding of the nature of the all-pervading relativism of the traditional Indian universe. The modern direction is towards the authoritarian, unambiguous centre in matters of belief, and we must suppose that those beliefs which more directly govern the ordering of caste relationships must alter conformably.

NOTES

1. In fact nothing is 'invariable' in this country. Sundarana provided me with my unique experience of a *ling* not so orientated. It was in a wall-shrine in the Brahman street and faced north. The Parvati figure was obviously in receipt of regular worship and the *ling* appeared to be neglected. The Brahmans could explain neither the orientation of the *ling* nor its neglect.
2. M. N. Srinivas, *Religion and Society among the Coorgs of South India*, Clarendon Press, 1952, *passim*; *Caste in India and other essays*, Bombay, 1962, Chap. 2; *Social Change in Modern India*, California, 1966, Chaps. 1 & 2.
3. The passage continues, 'For the historian, the human point of view is final.' It is no less so for the anthropologist. R. G. Collingwood, *The Idea of History*, Clarendon Press, 1946.

5

A Vaishnavite Sect—the way of grace

The ritual symbiosis, which is fading fast in Sundarana, has vanished in larger, wealthier villages where the more educated Patidar go so far, sometimes, as to dismiss the worship of, and even the belief in, *mātā* as an evil superstition. More secular interdependencies are breaking down as well. Kishor shaves daily with a safety razor, and has no need for the village Barber who continues to make his morning rounds of other houses. Surajben washes her own clothes and sends them once a month to the laundry in Petlad, where they can be properly bleached. The mills in Petlad employ more men than they did in the past, and the Patidar landlords have, perhaps for the first time ever, to compete for field labour, especially at sowing time and harvest. It is a sign of the times that the Untouchables, mostly of the Roman persuasion, thrive with their own co-operative society, and send their sons to the Jesuit college at Anand.

The buttresses of hierarchy collapse and Western technology obliterates both traditional services and goods. Each caste would survive in an increasing moral isolation were it not for the surrounding ambience of sects, which seem to come into their own in these circumstances.

Membership of a sect, adherence to a particular *guru* are not commonly incompatible with caste duties. Indeed, few sects have opposed caste regulations and survived. Sectarian teaching is adapted to man-in-the-world. Its profoundest inspiration may be the call to renunciation of the world, but this is tempered to the obligations surrounding the house-holder, who may admire this ideal while still supporting his wife and children. There are differences of emphasis accordingly as the sect is highly organized and explicit in its teaching, or amorphous, being the almost haphazard accumulation of disciples and admirers round one *guru*. In the former case there is a tendency (as I shall show) for the authority of caste rules to become contingent upon the permission or sanctioning authority of the sect. In the latter case the *guru's* teaching very often simply enforces the basic values of caste and his more transcendental teaching provides, as it were, a resting place at the side of the main road of caste where men walk.

I seem to note in highly organized sects a reduction of caste regulations such that, although still practised, they are endorsed by the theology of the sect. This is one way of looking at the situation. Equally we must recognize two developments: first, the authority of the sect strengthens these regulations when secular influences would otherwise weaken them, and secondly, if these secular influences do succeed, sect remains as almost the sole repository of caste values.

Here is a real irony. The sect, the individual *guru*, comes from and points towards the caste-transcending world. The message of renunciation is transmitted to the laity, provided that it accommodates the language and values of caste. In its turn the sect becomes the sole guardian of that language as the world of caste begins to fall apart.

The historical development sketched in the preceding paragraph sets in motion, I shall argue, a dialectic *within* the sect and between it and the modern, Western-influenced world.

This irony finds a parallel in the very foundation of the sect, for these movements succeed and survive precisely to the extent that they frustrate the initial ambitions of their founders. A man renounces the world and becomes a *sannyāsi* dedicated to the lonely pursuit of his spiritual truth. Such a man would, were he successful, remove himself more and more from the world of men and finally be lost to human sight. How does it come about, then, that sometimes he becomes the revered, often deified, head and founder of what we call a sect, with its own scriptures, rituals and temples?

Traditionally in India man's life is divided into four stages of development. First that of the unmarried student, *brahmachārya*. Students of Gandhi's life and writings will recognize this term as one which Gandhi used to apply to his own practice of strict chastity. The second stage is that of the married householder, *grahasthya*. This word still survives in very polite speech to mean 'gentleman'. The third stage is the least specific and is called *vānaprastha*. At this time of life a man should be thinking of withdrawing himself from worldly affairs prior to the final stage of *sannyāsa* when, ideally, he leaves house and kin and withdraws in pursuit of a purely spiritual goal.

Obviously the number of people who can ever have followed through this complete programme must have been limited. The majority of the population, in the past as now, must devote itself to getting a subsistence from early childhood to the cremation pyre. It is striking, nevertheless, that in the houses of the relatively affluent peasantry, the idea of some spiritual withdrawal in the last years of life is strong. Old men properly devote themselves to pilgrimage and meditation, even if they do not totally abandon the general oversight of their land or business.

Sannyāsa has come, through the centuries, to be a very different thing from the stage described in the old texts. It can be chosen by a man at any age and is achieved by initiation, *diksha*, from a preceptor who has himself been initiated. In this is implied a continuity of a philosophical tradition and to this extent we can recognize schools of *sannyāsi*. Some *sannyāsi* live in monasteries subject to particular rules, others are more individualistic in their pursuit, and travel widely throughout India.[1]

It is only realistic to recognize that this institution which evokes awe and respect from so many is sometimes abused and exploited. My own first sight of these 'holy men' corresponded perfectly to the average Westerner's expectations. Three such visited Sundarana, their long hair piled high on their heads, their loins girt with saffron-coloured cloth, their sturdy well-fed bodies marked with the insignia of Shiva. They wore heavy rosaries round their necks and carried strangely twisted staves. They were received, initially, with a cautious respect but, within forty-eight hours they were beaten up and chased out of the village. What they had done I could not clearly elicit, but it had something to do with women. Much later, in Dwāraka, the famous temple town on the west coast of Gujurat, I encountered a more sophisticated version. This was a young man who had dropped out of some university and operated with the smooth plausibility of any urban con-man. The local Brahmans, more experienced in this kind of thing, warned me before I had paid excessively. It was this young man who told me of the 'holy market' in Jāmnagar town where, on a certain day, the supposed *sannyāsi* met to swap and sell gifts received from the faithful.

While recognizing that all this can happen, two qualifying observations must be made. First of all, in a country where poverty is still so prevalent, who can blame those who, having no alternative but beggary, practise it in its most profitable garb? Secondly, my experience does not lead me to support a belief, common in some urban circles, that all *sannyāsi* are rogues. No one who has experienced that quality of serenity and power, which is felt almost as a physical emanation from the true *sannyāsi*, could suppose that this tradition is finally decadent.

Let me return to those ascetics who, paradoxically, originate sects. As I have indicated, their relative success in the

H

spiritual pilgrimage can attract others who come for guidance and initiation. In the biographies of saints one can read of such temporary groups, which break up when the preceptor himself feels it necessary to go on alone, or when his disciples feel they are ready, as individuals, to go. But it can happen that the group becomes permanent and, whether it settles in a forest or in a monastery, it then develops a fixed discipline, and the leadership is perpetuated by rules of spiritual succession.

This settling down, this institutionalization, however edifying its products, is strictly speaking a corruption of the world-rejecting *sannyāsic* ideal. The laity assist in this corruption precisely to the extent that it is at the same time edifying. Monasteries can accumulate large endowments from the benefactions of the faithful, and lay congregations accumulate around the *guru* and his immediate following. This is the result of what, in India, is sometimes called 'guru worship', the desire for spiritual guidance from some one enlightened soul.

In Gujarat today there are many households which revere some wandering *sannyāsi* as their family *guru* and preserve, perhaps, some souvenir of him, an eating dish, a sandal or even a footprint in red paint printed on paper, among their household gods. The holy man visits their town from time to time, conducts hymn singing and delivers sermons. When finally he dies his memory may be preserved but he does not necessarily leave any sect or order behind him. Some, however, leave amongst their disciples a desire to perpetuate their teachings and practice in some permanent form. Where there are wealthy patrons a piece of land may be set aside, a temple and accommodation for the brotherhood built, books of the *guru's* sayings together with exegeses of these sayings are published, rituals are elaborated, and for a few decades, or for centuries, the faithful come to regard the particular veneration of this *guru's* memory as their personal *marga* or way.

In Indian thought, there is no discontinuity, such as there is in the West, between the individual *ātma*, soul, of the individual man and the ultimate *ātma* which governs and sustains the universe; it is therefore easy for the peasantry, following in the steps of the great man's earliest disciples, to equate him with, elevate him to, the status of godhead. The followers of Vallabhachārya today commonly refer to him as Mahā Prabhuji, revered great god (see below, p. 108).

Clearly, membership of a sect can mean different things according to the particular way in which the essential fact, the relationship with the *guru*, is mediated. The most diffuse form is indicated by such terms as Vaishnavism and Shivaism which imply theologies and philosophies centring respectively, but not necessarily exclusively, on Vishnu and Shiva. A man may well call himself a Vaishnavite because his family traditionally visits the god in his house. Such a man can scarcely be said to have a *guru* other than the head of his favourite temple, whom he may revere in the most general sense.

Somewhat less diffuse is the situation in which the head of a temple, or some holy man attached to it, attracts congregations of pilgrims on holy days and instructs them in the simplified theology of one of the great Vaishnavite philosophers (see below, p. 109). Regular members of this congregation count themselves as having received *diksha*, or initiation from this particular *guru* and wear a particular kind of necklace, *kanthi*, made of *tulsi, occimum sanctum*, Holy Basil. The term *diksha* can mean initiation in this loose sense although properly it means the awakening of spiritual potential by, usually, the imparting of a sacred and secret phrase, *mantra*.

Altogether more formal, and corresponding much more to what sectarian membership connotes in English, is the acceptance of a precise way of life, particular devotional reading, and the authority, even in secular matters, of the head, or his representative, of a particular body having its own temples, rituals and the like, and a sect mark which its members paint on the brow. Such membership still differs from the membership of a Church or Nonconformist 'sect' in that, despite common rituals, liturgy and rules, there is still considerable emphasis upon submission to one particular guide within the body of the movement, who is accepted as the individual layman's *guru*.

In the pages that follow I shall be giving examples of the origin and history of particular sects and the organization of their membership. Towards the end I shall argue, from one particular example, that it is precisely the extent to which the central importance of this *guru* relationship is lost, or minimized, by an over-emphasis upon solidarity, organization and uniformity, that the sect appears to lose its hold upon the population of the modern Indian city. It seems most significant to me, and I hope to succeed in conveying this, that '*guru* worship', that is the selection by individuals of holy preceptors, often living at a great distance, is said to be on the increase in city populations.

Before I discuss particular sects I must revert to Sundarana to examine the word *bhakti*, usually translated as devotion, which is, together with the *guru*, an essential ingredient of sectarian life and philosophy.

The word devotion adequately translates *bhakti* but, particularly in popular usage and in certain schools of thought, *bhakti* carries also associations of enthusiasm, fervour and love which the English word has perhaps lost. Let me quote a few verses from the *Bhakti Sutras* of Devarsi Narada: 'Bhakti is supreme love directed towards God; it is nectar and this nectar brings self-realization through total satisfaction . . . The realization of *bhakti* in the form of the Supreme Love, makes man mad, silent and lost in the delight of the *ātma*.' The Srimad Bhāgavata, a *purāna* of wide acceptance among Vaishnavites, describes as follows the behaviour of the *bhakta*, devotee: '[he] loses all sense of decorum . . . and, like one possessed, he now bursts into peals of laughter, now weeps, now cries, now sings aloud and now begins to dance in a singular way.'[2]

This is a use of imagery familiar to the student of Christian and other mysticisms, which speak of the soul as being mad or intoxicated with love. Obviously one rarely sees people in such a condition. At the same time it is worth noting that in temple rituals and hymn-singing in India there are more smiles, and altogether a greater sense of people enjoying themselves, than are found in Western churches.

Strangely enough I first heard the word *bhakti* in circumstances corresponding more closely to the poetic description than I was ever to see again.

It was shortly after I had settled at Sundarana. Early one morning I was standing on the steps of the bungalow which looked on to the lane running up to the village, and noticed an old man ambling along chatting animatedly to himself. As he came closer it was apparent that he was speaking to God, Bhagvān, the very commonest word for the deity in this area. He had a small bunch of flowers in his hand which he scattered as he walked, and he was trying, at the same time, to pick the odd flower out of the thorn hedge by his side. In this attempt he pricked himself and held his finger up saying 'O, Bhagvān, look what you have done to me, for you I would throw myself into the thorn hedge.' He did not throw himself into the thorn hedge and gently made his way back to the village. I turned to Momad and asked what all that had been about. 'It's *bhakti*,' he said, 'he is showing his love for the Lord Krishna.' Momad also went on to explain that the man did no work, only came home to drink tea, and was generally a great source of worry and nuisance to his family.

The doctrine of *bhakti*, the belief in the all-saving power of devotion, is widespread throughout India. The European can find its most famous exposition in the Bhagavadagita. This text is, naturally enough, available in Gujarati

for a rupee or two, and the complicated teaching is sometimes read out in the evenings for the edification of the
villagers. Even in the Gujarati the language is of a highly
elevated nature and tends to prefer the Sanskrit derived and
scholarly term to the more simple language of the village. It
is questionable whether the fine distinction between, for
example, the manifest and the unmanifest are seized in all
their complexity. Again, the villagers' understanding seems
to be selective in that, for example, the stress which this
text lays upon the renunciation of the fruits of action tends
to be lost to sight. Certainly the lowest common denominator
of the beliefs about *bhakti* in Sundarana combines emotion
with a lack of ethical or social restraint. Two famous verses
are often cited:

> Even a man of the vilest conduct who worships me with a
> single mind must be reckoned holy, for he has decided
> rightly. (IX verse 30)
> Those who seek my protection, whether they are sinners,
> women, Vaishya or Shudra, will all achieve the highest
> heaven. (IX verse 32)

I have been assured that these are to be taken at their face
value; for a more moralistic view the reader should see
Radakrishnan's translation and gloss of these verses.[3] It
is perhaps worth noting that in the second verse Radakrishnan gives 'lowly born' for *papayonayah*; the Sanskrit
term suggests 'born of sin' and hence 'sinful', as the
Gujarati translations frankly render it.

The wandering devotee of the kind that I have described
is of course rare. The most common manifestation of *bhakti*
in the village is found in the *bhajan mandali*, hymn-singing
groups. In theory, as the doctrine of *bhakti* suggests, there
are no caste distinctions to the membership of these groups
and, indeed, none are exclusive in theory. In fact those
Untouchables in the village who have not succumbed to the
Christian mission have their own group.

In Sundarana there were two such *bhajan mandali*. The first was predominantly Patidar, but it also included some Bareia and members of artisan castes. It also included the muslim Momad, interestingly enough, although some of his relatives, vague though they were about the implications of Islam, were somewhat uneasy about his attendance. The second group was predominantly Patanwadia, but had members from all other castes excluding, of course, the Untouchables and, I think, the Patidar.

Of the two groups the second one appeared to be the more cohesive and regularly active. The instruments had been purchased entirely by communal subscription. In the Patidar group the essential instruments were for the most part privately owned; quarrels occasionally broke out if the owner of an important instrument was not disposed to sit up all night but would not lend his instrument to someone else.

The Patidar group owned a large stock of cymbals and other percussion instruments, including the hollow brass rods which are clashed together by the participants in the folk dance, *ras*, which has now become only an occasional feature of village life. This dance, which is believed to be the one danced by Krishna with his shepherd girls, is still danced with vigour and grace in Saurashtra and Kutch, but the performances which I witnessed in Central Gujarat were tame affairs, more resembling well-disciplined sound and movement exercises than an exciting and potentially erotic dance.

The purpose of the *bhajan mandali* is, as the name indicates, to sing hymns, and sessions are usually held in the winter when there is less work to do in the fields. Like most musical performances in India, it takes several hours for the performers, here the entire congregation, to get into the spirit of the thing, and the sessions usually last all night. The *bhajan* are devotional and moral in content. The ideal that they hold up is of the soul lovesick and lonely waiting only for a sight of the divine lover. Traditionally they praise the practice of *bhakti* as superior to rituals in the pursuit of salvation, point sometimes to the folly of the external signs and formalities of the priesthood, and even occasionally criticize the distinctions which society has made between men.

The tradition of *bhajan* writing still goes on today and cheap editions of modern *bhajan* set to popular film tunes are commonly available in most bazaars. The *bhajan* of two great fifteeenth-century devotees are also still sung. Narsinha Mehta and Mirabai, who composed these *bhajan*, are also remembered as examples of the devout life. Of Narsinha there is a story to the effect that, following the precepts of the Gita, he shared his devotional practices with Untouchables. As a result he was outcasted by his fellow Nāgar Brahmans, a Brahman caste still very highly regarded and, until quite recently, very influential in Gujarat. As he was outcasted Narsinha was not allowed to join in communal feasts, and the story goes that as they sat down to dine the Lord Krishna made it seem to them that beside each Brahman an Untouchable was sitting.

Mirabai is famous throughout India for her contribution to this kind of literature. She is said to have been a Rajput princess and many dramatic tales are told about her. In her *bhajan* she figures herself variously as the slave, wife and even mother of the Lord Krishna. The following translation of part of a *bhajan* written by a famous devotee Dayaram (1767–1852) brings out strongly the erotic imagery.

> Do come over to my house, Prince darling,
> Do come over to my house. Come, come there to drink
> And make me drink
> The cup of love; Then shall ride the steed of your youth.
> At nightfall come, my darling dear, for none shall find
>   out then.[4]

When the *bhajan mandali* is meeting and is in full swing, it is clear that the participants are thoroughly emotionally involved in their performance. It is not uncommon for those who may not be singing to interject praises of the sentiments being expressed. However, we should no more expect that the singers are paying attention to the theology of the *bhajan* than we expect the average English churchgoer to be concerned with the theology, more or less clearly expressed, in the hymns which he too enjoys singing. Like most people involved in choral singing the participants enjoy the sense of community and the sound of their music more than either meaning or imagery. There is nothing more ludicrous about a group of grizzled and burly Patidar farmers singing of themselves as lovesick shepherdesses than there is about a Welsh male voice choir singing 'O love that will not let me go'. I never heard anybody suggest that the ritual and caste-transcending message of the *bhajan* should be put into practice.

The Patidar and the men of Sundarana in general are not great temple-goers, especially during their active lives. It is considered quite proper, however, for an elderly man to indulge in devotions which might call for amused criticism were he still young. Such a man might go to offer flowers to *Mahādev* once or twice a day, read devotional books and carry a rosary with him. Such men would be almost bound to be members of respectable, that is to say wealthy, families because otherwise they could not afford the leisure. If their circumstances make them respectable then they may well be addressed by others as *bhagat*, devotee. However, I should point out that the term *bagbhagat*, pseudo-*bhagat* or hypocrite, is not uncommonly used in the village.

Although the average villager may not be very active in devotional matters, small-scale pilgrimages are another matter. The day of the full moon, *punam*, is regarded as the holiest day of any lunar month and the most appropriate time for visiting a temple. This is the only regular excuse for an outing and, for many, it is the only opportunity that they have of seeing a little of the outside world. There are, of course, important shrines in other villages, but in this part of Gujarat there is no more famous temple than the Temple of Dakor, and the local railway authority puts on special trains for pilgrims at the full moon. The temple at Dakor derives its sanctity from the presence of an image of the Lord Krishna, under the name Ranchodji, which, it is believed, came from the temple, famous throughout India, of Dwāraka on the coast of Saurashtra. It is believed that the temple at Dwāraka was built by the Lord Krishna himself.

The story of the image of Ranchodji is interesting because it provides an example of the way in which the spiritual properties of one place can be appropriated by another; Dakor is in many ways in rivalry with Dwāraka as a centre of pilgrimage. It is said that Bodāno, a great devotee to the Lord Krishna, once lived in what was then the village of Dakor. He was so devoted to the Lord that he allowed a *tulsi* plant, sacred to Krishna, to grow in the palm of his hand, and made it a practice to walk the two or three hundred miles to the temple at Dwāraka once a year. When he grew too old to travel in this way he was bitterly upset, but the Lord Krishna appeared to him in a dream assuring him that if he would make the journey once more he, Krishna, would return with him to Dakor. Bodāno set out on the journey and, with the assistance of his Lord, was able to steal the image and bring it home with him. The story is well known throughout Gujarat and there are different places between Dwāraka and Dakor marking the resting places of the image.

The loss did not long pass unnoticed and the temple of Brahmans finally tracked the image to Dakor. By this time Bodāno had died and his widow was guarding it. The Lord Krishna appeared to her and told her not to be afraid, but to go out to the temple Brahmans and ask them which they would prefer, the image itself or its weight in gold. The greedy Brahmans preferred the gold and a balance was brought. The image was placed in one pan and the widow, advised by Krishna, threw into the other a small gold ear-ring which immediately outweighed the image. The Brahmans retired outwitted back to Dwāraka, where, rather to my surprise, their descendants still tell the tale today.

Vaishnavism provides the idiom for what seems to be a special area of Gujarati social life, a section in which universalist values can be expressed through the *bhajan*, and individualistic values asserted through *bhakti*. Instead of obliging us to see, as *shaktipuja* does, purity and impurity, Brahman and Untouchable, linked by a symbiosis which makes this life meaningful, this language speaks of an equality brought about by each individual's dedication to a single lord.

Once again we are not dealing with a real contradiction in social life, however contradictorv the two doctrines may appear to us. In part the problem relates back to the discussion about ghosts and rebirth: it is perfectly possible for an individual to believe that his devotion to the Lord will bring him release from re-birth, heaven or whatever after-life he conceives, and still believe simultaneously in re-birth for others.

I asked Kishor to explain the law of *karma* to me and he explained it very much as it appears in the popular texts: a man is re-born in a condition which fits his actions in this present existence. At the same time a man is obliged to act according to the law of his temperament and could not, therefore, avoid sin if his nature was sinful. I tried to get him to speak of free will which seemed to me to be the essence of the *bhakti* doctrine. Kishor, quite rightly I now think, shut me up with: 'These are all the affairs of Bhagvān. One does what one can.' The situation was as absurd as that of an agnostic quizzing the average church-goer in this country on such mysteries as the relation of God's infinite mercy to His infinite justice, and the 'problem of evil' in the light of God's omniscience and omnipotence.

Before I give my understanding of the significance of

Vaishnavism I should say something of its emergence in this part of India. The word Vaishnavism does not mean solely the worship of Vishnu because this has always been there, associated with the earliest Shivaite temples. By Vaishnavism I mean that cult which puts Vishnu firmly at the centre, and by Vaishnavism in Gujarat I mean the Vaishnavism that chooses Krishna as the divine embodiment.

Two immensely influential characters were born within a few years of each other towards the end of the fifteenth century. The first of these was later known as Vallabhachārya, *achārya* being the honorific title suffixed to the name of philosopher teachers. He was born somewhere in what is now called Madhya Pradesh while his parents were fleeing from a rumoured Muslim invasion of Banares where the family had originated. The second was Chaitanya Deva who was born in Bengal. Vallabhachārya in the west and Chaitanya in the east initiated Vaishnavite movements that still characterize these areas. Both have been deified by subsequent tradition, and it is impossible now to sort out the facts of their early lives and intentions. Two facts of some importance are, however, certain. Neither of these teachers appears to have had any intention of founding a church or sect. They seem rather to have been wandering scholars who attracted a following around them. Indeed, as far as Chaitanya is concerned the word scholar is possibly not appropriate; he is traditionally regarded as more of a devotee than a thinker. However, the traditions of both movements credit Chaitanya's chief disciple Nityananda and Vallabhachārya's son Vitthaleshwara with the subsequent organization and theological development of the two movements. It is also important to note that the lifetimes of these two men and the succeeding decades fell in a period of increasing upheaval, particularly in northern India, as the Mogul empire established itself.[5]

India had suffered Muslim invasion from the eighth century onwards. Still today Mahmud of Ghazni, or Mahmud

Begadda, the eleventh-century iconoclast, is remembered in Gujarat for his destruction of the famous temple of Somnath, dedicated to Shiva, on the Saurashtrian coast. From the ninth century onwards the indigenous institutions and beliefs of India were subjected to the first impact of a monotheist absolutism. Vallabhachārya and Chaitanya are only two in a series of famous men, some devotees, some teachers, who sprang up from the eleventh century onwards. Among these are Rāmanujachāraya who preached in south India the unity of the divine in the form of Vishnu; his successor Rāmananda who carried his faith to the north; Kabir, disciple of a devotional mysticism; the famous Nanak, a little older than Chaitanya and Vallabhachārya, who in the fifteenth century initiated the movement known today as Sikhism.

The distinctive tradition of Vaishnavite philosophy is associated with the thought of four influential Vaishnava *achārya*: Rāmanuja, Nimbarka, Madhva, and Vishnu Swāmi. The followers of Vallabhachārya tend to substitute his name for that of Vishnu Swāmi as the fourth of the great teachers, and in fact he appears to have derived much of his doctrine from the Swāmi's philosophy. Despite considerable differences between them, what these teachers have in common is a reaction to the dominating teaching of Shankachārya, the philosopher credited with re-establishing in the eighth century pure Brahmanic orthodoxy over against Buddhism.

What Shankara actually taught and how he is popularly represented are two different things. Just as most people in the West have a few tag ideas which they associate with Plato, Aquinas, or Marx, so Shivaism and monism characterize Shankaracharya. It is indeed probable that Shivaism provided him with his theological idiom, and certain that his successors today associate themselves in worship with Shiva rather than with Vishnu; his philosophy goes far beyond such identifications. The simplest expression of monism is this:

There exists one spirit alone, and the feelings of individuality and other attributes of the animal spirit and the
variety of the inanimate world, owe their origin to a
principle of illusion, and are consequently unreal.[6]

Although modern followers of Shankachārya maintain that
he included *bhakti* in his system, which he may well have
done, it can perhaps be seen that this doctrine of monism, of
advaita, unity, undividedness, is incompatible with the idea
of devotion, in that both the feelings of the devotee and the
object of his devotion are illusory, *maya*. Out of the teaching
of the Vaishnav *achārya* there grew immensely complicated
theories, all claiming support from the Upanishads, which
gave some kind of autonomy to the individual souls. Because
all these teachers never questioned the ultimate priority and
unity of Brahma, their theories are not to be called anti-
monist but rather modified monisms. Vallabhachārya called
his own philosophy Shudhadvaita, pure monism, or monism
correctly understood.

I quote some verses from one of the few works attributed
to Vallabhachārya, the *Tattwarthadipanibandha*:

15. In this Kali Yuga [dark age] God having incarnated
himself as Buddha, the gods who minister to the latter
incarnate themselves in the form of Brahmans who delude
the people by spreading various kinds of errors and thus
prevent them from worshipping Krishna.
27. By the mere desire which was expressed by the words
'May I be many' souls arose as so many parts of Brahman.
29. From the joy-form of God came out the in-dwelling
spirits which have in them the three attributes of God,
being (*sat*), consciousness (*chit*) and joy (*ananda*). The
jiva (individual souls) are without joy, and matter is without joy and consciousness.
30. Therefore the *jiva* are without joy. Matter, *jiva*, and
in-dwelling souls are thus different in nature though they
are all made of one god.

36. By the manifestation of the part of joy in himself, the soul attains Brahman-bhava (divinity) and fellowship with God. These can be attained only by the worship of Hari (Krishna).

42. The love with a full knowledge of the glory of God, which is, besides, well established and surpasses all other kinds of love, is called *bhakti*. This alone gives salvation, and nothing else.

87. If the universe be accepted as illusory, salvation becomes an unreality like the elephant seen in a dream. The creation of the universe by *maya* . . . is contrary to the teaching of the Vedas and the Brahma Sutras.

89. The illusory character of the universe taught by the Puranas is only for the purpose of wakening the sense of detachment from the world. To say, therefore, that the universe is the result of *avidya*, ignorance, is to mislead one.[7]

The great Sanskritist, Sir Ramkrishna Gopal Bhandarkar, comments as follows:

The whole world has Brahman for its material cause. The perception of forms apparently different from the Brahman is due to ignorance or delusion and to the true nature of Brahman being rendered imperceptible. The individual soul is identical with Brahman, a part of Brahman and atomic. From the *aksara* (which is the ultimate Brahma) composed of existence, intelligence and joy (*saccidananda*) particles come out as sparks from fire. From the predominance of the *sat* (existence) portion in them the joy portion is concealed, and thus we have the individual souls possessing *sat*, existence, and *cit*, intelligence. The individual soul is not a form of the Supreme Soul altered by a third thing being involved in it, such as the Maya (illusive power), but is itself the same substance as the Supreme Soul with one attribute rendered imperceptible. The relation between the two is thus that of identity (*advaita*), both being in the pristine unchanged form, i.e. identity of untransformed souls (suddhadvaita).[8]

I have quoted from Vallabhachārya and Bhandarkar at some length in order to give a sample of the kinds of distinction made in traditional Indian theology and philosophy. The thought being expressed by these two writers is relatively simple as compared with some expositions.

One element in Vallabhachārya's teaching needs to be added. The sect is called the Pushti Marga, the Way of Grace, and Vallabhachārya laid particular stress upon the *pushti*, grace of Krishna, in bringing the soul, according to its abilities, to a closer and closer devotion.

Vallabhachārya departed from the world in 1532. Some traditions maintain that before his death he went through the formal rites of renunciation and became a *sannyāsi*. Others vehemently deny this and insist that, in death as in life, Vallabhachārya had no use for austerity and renunciation. H. H. Wilson records the tradition of his end as follows:

Vallabha is supposed to have closed his career in a miracle: he had finally settled at Jethan Ber, at Banaras, near which a Math (monastery) still subsists, but at length, having accomplished his mission, he is said to have entered the Ganges at Hanuman Ghat, when, stooping into the water, he disappeared: a brilliant flame arose from the spot, and, in the presence of a host of spectators, he ascended to Heaven and was lost in the firmament.[9]

Vallabhachārya's successor was his younger son variously known as Vitthaleshwara, Vitthalnatha, or Goswami, cow protector. He appears to have enjoyed considerable royal patronage during his lifetime, including that of the emperor Akbar. When he died he left an image of the Lord Krishna to each of his seven sons from whom the Maharajas of today are descended. The eldest son received the image which, it was believed, had been presented to Vallabhachārya by the

Lord Himself, and the *haveli* in which this image is established, at Nāthadwāra in Rajasthan, is the most sacred place
of the entire sect.

The particular teachings of Vallabhachārya need not
concern us, but subsequent writers have tended to equate
him with Luther on two scores: first it is said that he pinned
up on a temple door in Banares the grounds of his argument
against the prevailing philosophy of Shankarachya; and
secondly because of his emphasis, already alluded to, upon
enjoyment of the things of the world. For Vallabhachārya it
seems, as for Luther, man could only exalt the glory of God
by appreciating to the full his own sinfulness. Vallabhachārya's teaching was more fully expounded and enriched
by his grandson, Vitthaldās, who also was responsible for
designing the elaborate domestic ritual of the sect.

Officially the sect has no temples, although to the outsider
it appears to have many which are both rich and complex.
What seem to be temples are, according to the sectarians,
the private mansions, *haveli*, of the Maharajahs in which
they live with the image, *murti*, of the Lord Krishna. The
daily ritual in which the god is bathed, dressed, fed,
entertained and finally put to bed are thought of as part of
the domestic life of the Maharaja which the faithful are
allowed to witness.

Although the sect appears to have passed its luxurious
heyday in the nineteenth century it is still very large and
influential. The present Maharajas and their followers are
quite excessively sensitive to the reported delinquencies of
their grandfathers; for this reason some are reticent about
the doctrines and practices of the sect. I am, understandably,
very grateful therefore to the present incumbent of the
Kankroli *haveli*, Shri Vrajbhushanlalji Maharaj who, to my
mind, embodies the spirit of the Pushti Marga.

He is a tall, well-built man in his mid-fifties, very fair and
fresh complexioned. He is a scholar who, unlike some of his
brethren, has published in Hindi extensive works on the

Kankroli *haveli,* and the teachings of his ancestor. In addition to many audiences, he also allowed me to sit as often and as long as I liked at the foot of the *murti,* and to watch the ritual. What stands out most clearly in my memory of him is the very jollity, I can think of no better word, which he brought to these acts. Whatever he was doing, whether feeding the god, giving him a toy, or, the most solemn moment of the day, offering him the evening incense, *ārati,* the almost irresistible illusion was that here a father was performing services for a loved son whose every need and movement was a source of delight to him.

In one formal audience, I asked him why the adolescent form of the Lord Krishna had been selected for worship by the sect, and his reply was characteristic: 'Well, you know, supposing that we were to worship the Lord [Krishna] in his mature form as king, how should we dare to lay down the rules for him? We couldn't say to him "Now you're going to eat this and now you're going to wear that", and we certainly couldn't pack him off to bed at six o'clock in the evening.' This remark produced a wave of laughter among the people sitting around us, and on me a sense of what Christianity had lost by its simple-minded interpretation of image worship, and subsequent condemnation of it. Christianity has no conception of *maya,* the play/illusion of the apparent world. The Western mind pursues the ineffable to trap it in words. Each successive conceptualization becomes exactly that proximate, *maya,* with which, exactly, it cannot settle down and live.

The teaching of the Pushti Marga, to the effect that nothing in life was bad, or rather that all could be made good by being offered to Krishna, was clearly an appealing one. The *haveli* in the various parts of western India became immensely wealthy as gifts poured in to the Maharaja and to the image.

It is not possible even to estimate the membership of the sect at its height at the end of the nineteenth century. One of the main seats of the sect was in Surat in south Gujarat; in addition there were minor seats in Baroda and at Dwāraka on the west coast. The island of Bet off the coast from Dwāraka was a famous centre devoted by the sectarians to the enactment of the life of Krishna as king. Temples were erected to his wives, whose priests, dressed as women, took their turns in performing the *seva puja*, service-worship, of the god. There are old men alive today who remember the glories of Bet Dwāraka, as it is known, but now the temples are largely deserted, and the mansions of the Bhātia merchant-princes have their shutters permanently closed.

More important than the number of those who wore the *kanthi*, necklace, of the Maharajas is the influence of the sect in shaping the temple worship of Vaishnavites throughout Gujarat. Even at Dwāraka, one of the main seats of Shankachārya's spiritual successors, the elaborate ritual performed daily throughout the day in the temple is conducted along the lines laid down by one of Vallabhachārya's descendants, even though the temple priests themselves do not admit the authority of the Maharajas. At Dakor also the temple worship derives from the same inspiration.

The key word in this kind of worship is *seva*, service. The idea is that the image is an embodiment, *svarupa*, true form, of the Lord Krishna. The priest is a servant in the house of this Lord and performs the daily services which such a king, or royal prince, requires.

The Lord's day is divided into eight parts when appropriate *seva* is made. It is only at these times that the laity may have a sight, *darshan*, of their Lord. The word *darshan* connotes more than a mere perception; it is a benediction to the seer. It is considered beneficial not only to have *darshan* of images but also of holy and great men, and this is a rather disconcerting belief for the Westerner. It is not uncommon for one to be ushered into the presence of some *guru*, visiting *sannyāsi*, or other respected teacher, and then just to sit for ten to fifteen minutes in a silence which may only be broken by the great man himself asking a few questions, usually through someone else, about one's origins and interests.

The first main *seva* of the day is called *mangala* and takes place early in the morning when the god is awakened. The second, *sringāra*, shows the image fully dressed. The third, called *gvāla*, represents the image as prepared to go out to graze the cattle. The fourth, one of the major occasions for *darshan*, is known as *rājabhoga*, when large dishes of specially prepared foods are presented to the image and subsequently distributed as *prasād*. After this meal the image is believed to take a siesta and the fifth occasion for *darshan* is called *utthapana* when he is awakened. This is followed by another meal called simply *bhoga*. The seventh *darshan*, *sandhya*, represents the Lord as returning from the pasture. This is followed by the last *darshan*, *shayana*, when the image goes to sleep. This last *darshan* of the day is another major occasion for the laity; at this time *ārati*, incense, is offered to the image before it retires.

Apart from what the faithful see when the temple doors are open, the image is the object of priestly activity almost throughout the day. Food of some kind is offered at every *darshan* and this must be prepared in special kitchens. The bathing and the dressing of the image also take place when the temple doors are closed. Rather as in the Catholic church, but with very much more variety, colours, foods, clothes and jewellery of the image vary according to the season.

The treasuries of some images are astonishing. Through the years the faithful have not only presented utensils of silver and gold but also jewelled tiaras, necklets, bracelets and anklets. Quite often a wealthy devotee will pay for the *rājbhoga* offering to the god and, to do himself credit, this will be an offering of the most expensive dishes that Indian cuisine can provide. A further source of income is the offering made by the devotee when he receives the *prasād*.

I intend to give elsewhere a fuller account of *seva puja*, but I hope to have said enough to convey something of the

spirit and the sight of this form of worship. It is, as it is
intended to be, at once homely and royal. The philosophy
behind it is undemanding and requires simple mental dedication to a physical object and the giving of gifts. More
than any other sect in Gujarat, the Pushti Marga provided
an arena in which the wealthy merchant classes could
display their wealth and earn at once distinction and merit.
It is not surprising that the Bhātia of Kutch, who appear to
have sprung from relatively humble origins as coastal traders
and fishermen, were happy to devote themselves *tan, man,
dhan*, mind, body and property, to the worship of the
Maharajas. Sir Richard Burton witnessed the reaction of
the Bhātia in Zanzibar to a Maharaja who visited them in the
1850s. He records that in return for their oblations the
Maharaja pardoned them for their sin in dealing in cattle
hides, and it seems certain that, for the Bhātia at least, the
Pushti Marga was also the way of social status.[10]

It would be wrong to say that the Pushti Marga is on the
decline today, but it has certainly to face a strong rival in
the form of the Satsang, the Society of the True, which was
founded by Swāmi Narāyan in the nineteenth century. The
Satsang was formed, if not in opposition to the Pushti Marga,
at least as a corrective to some aspects of it. It seems clear
that, perhaps especially in the nineteenth century, certain
abuses crept into the practices of the latter sect.

One can often find references in the literature of the
'notorious Maharaj libel case' which, authors assume, was so
notorious that no further details are required. The suggestion
is of such licentiousness and unnameable abominations that
I think it is worth setting down the simple facts of the
matter. It seems a great pity that still today members of the
Pushti Marga are over-sensitive about events which occurred
over a century ago, and are still contaminated in memory by
the reactions of the then middle classes in Gujarat, who
participated with their British rulers 'in one of their
periodical fits of morality'.

At about the mid-point of the nineteenth century some of the Maharajas of the Pushti Marga were in dispute with local Brahmans in Bombay about the perquisites of a certain temple. This dispute spread to other matters, and since the Maharajas were already unpopular with the reformist middle classes, the cause of the Bombay Brahmans was taken up by the local press and a campaign was launched against the sect and its leaders.

A leading reformer was Karshandas Mulji, a Gujarati Bania, editor of the newspaper *Satya Prakash*, the Light of Truth, founded in 1855 for the general purpose of furthering religious and social reforms, and for the particular purpose of attacking the Maharajas.[11]

The *Satya Prakash* was only one of several vernacular newspapers dedicated to similar general ends.[12] For the Maharajas the particular sting lay in the fact that Karshandas Mulji was, at least nominally, one of their own following. On 21 October 1860 he wrote and published an article accusing the Maharajas of 'shamelessness, subtlety, immodesty, rascality and deceit'; more particularly he accused them of adultery with the wives and daughters of their devotees.

The challenge was taken up by Jadunāthji Brijratanji, Maharaja of Surat, in south Gujarat. After public discussions and much delay he finally filed an action for libel against both the editor and the printer at the *Satya Prakash* on 14 May 1861. The Maharaja did not get off to a good start: once the defendants' pleas had been entered, he, or others on his behalf, set out to suborn witnesses. The sect was largely dependent upon the support of one caste in particular, the Bhātia caste, which, centred in Kutch, had grown immensely wealthy through the East African trade. The elders of this caste in Bombay sent out an order to the effect that no member of the caste should give evidence against the Maharaja; anyone so doing would be excommunicated. As soon as this fact was known the Bhātia elders were liable for a charge of conspiracy and the opportunity was seized by

Karshandas Mulji. At what came to be known as the Bhātia Conspiracy Case, the defendants were found guilty and fined a thousand rupees apiece.

The Maharaj Libel Case came up in January 1862 and lasted for forty days. Some thirty witnesses were called by each side, and among those for the defendants was the Reverend Dr. John Wilson, F.R.S., Honorary President of the Bombay branch of the Royal Asiatic Society. The discussion ranged over many matters of theology: were the Maharajas truly divine or not; was the sect in accordance with Vedic principles etc.; primarily it centred on the alleged immorality of the sect's doctrines and the particular immorality of the Maharajas.

Unlike many sects which had and have an essential ascetic inspiration, the sect of the Maharajas was designed more for life in the world, and placed great emphasis upon enjoying the things of the world. The worship of the sect centred upon Krishna in the form of a young boy, a lover adored by the Gopi, the shepherdesses. In evidence Dr. Wilson said that from his personal study of the doctrines of the sect, he believed them to be of an impure character. He admitted both that he had never been inside one of the temples, or personally observed 'improper practices' by the Maharajas; but he went on to say: 'I have seen very obscene conduct on the part of the followers of the Maharajas, and have turned away from it with disgust.' The nature of the immorality imputed to the Maharajas varied from pressing the toes of female devotees to having intercourse with them. It was alleged that members of the Bhātia sect in particular felt that they should offer their newly-wed brides to the Maharaja before enjoying them themselves. Dr. Wilson made a significant connexion between the worshippers of this sect and the worshippers of the 'female energies' as he called them, the Shaktis.[13] At the end of the case the judges were not entirely agreed on some points of law, but the final outcome was certainly a moral victory for Karsandas Mulji, who was also awarded costs. Sir Matthew Sausse concluded his judgement as follows: 'After having found a verdict for the defendants upon the issues raised by the plea of justification, the plaintiff can only recover a verdict for nominal damages on the plea of not guilty. As we have felt obliged to disbelieve the plaintiff on his oath and also a greater number of the witnesses produced to corroborate him, our verdict will be entered without costs.' These nominal damages were assessed at five rupees which, the Maharajas' party announced after the trial, was a gesture of compassion on the part of the court for the poverty of the defendant.

The English press in India was united in deploring the legal technicality which had prevented a total victory for Mulji. It went on to wag the finger of reproof, for example, the *Bombay Gazette*, 22 April 1862:

> If the natives have any respect for the opinions of their European acquaintances and friends, the knowledge on their part that the latter are now aware of the disgusting and abominable things that are done of them in secret, must have a salutary effect upon them. We call upon them to renounce these hidden works of darkness etc.

The *Bombay Saturday Review* spoke of 'loathsome lewdness' and inevitably, 'debasing bondage'. Many papers predicted great advantages for Christianity out of the trial, while the *Indian Banner*—'Oh! it shocks our feelings to speak more particularly of the impurities coming from the filthy flesh'— promised its readers that when a work on the *History of Civilization in India* came to be written, the account of the trial would constitute its 'raciest' chapter![14]

NOTES

1. For a general survey of *sādhu* see G. S. Ghurye, *Indian Sadhus*, Bombay, 1953. This reference calls to mind the memory of Dr. L. N. Chapekar whose sensitive assiduity as a field-worker enriched this, as many, of Ghurye's works.
2. *The Philosophy of Love—Bhakti-Sutras of Devarsi Narada*, edited by Hanuman Prasad Poddar. sixth edition, Gorakhpur, 1957, verses 1, 2, 3, 4 and 6, pp. 25–36.
3. *The Bhagavadgita*, edited by S. Radhakrishnan, London, 1948. On verse 30 this editor stresses the need for repentance accompanying the devotion. On verse 32 he insists that it 'is not to be regarded as supporting the social customs debarring women and Sudras from Vedic study . . . The Gita does not sanction these social rules. The Gita gets beyond racial distinctions in its emphasis on spiritual values.' See pp. 250–3.
4. N. A. Thoothi, *The Vaishnavites of Gujarat*, Calucutta, 1935, p. 258. This classical study gives other examples; see also *Vaishnava Lyrics*, done into English by Surendranath Kumar *et al.*, Oxford, 1923.
5. Bhai Manilal C. Parekh, *Sri Vallabhacharya*, Rajkot, 1943; M. T. Kennedy, *The Chaitanya Movement*, Calcutta, 1925; H. H. Wilson, *The Religious Sects of the Hindus*, 2nd edition, 1958.
6. Sir Ramkrishna Gopal Bandakar, *Vaisnavism, Saivism and minor religious systems*, edited by Narayan Bapuji Utgikar, Poona, 1928, p. 72.
7. Parekh, op. cit., 1946, Appendix II.
8. Bhandakar, op. cit., p. 110.
9. Wilson, op. cit., p. 69.
10. Sir Richard Burton, *Zanzibar, City and Island*, London, 1872.
11. Karshandas Mulji published anonymously his *History of the Maharajas, or Vallabhacharyas in Western India* (London, 1865) in which details of the case, reports of the judgements delivered, and press reactions thereto, are preceded by a most tendentious account of Hinduism in general, and of the Pushti Marga in particular.
12. For a succinct account of the emergence of a socially critical press in Gujarat, see R. D. Parikh, *The Press and Society*, Bombay, 1965.
13. My suggestion here is that the Bhattia may, on their conversion to the Pushti Marga, have brought with them elements of their older adherence. H. H. Wilson, op. cit., p. 138, writing of Shaktipuja, says: 'one of the principal rites . . . is the actual worship of the daughter or wife of a Brahman, and leads with one branch of the sect at least to the introduction of gross impurities.' See *History of the Sect of the Maharajas*, pp. 20, 30.
14. *History of the Sect of the Maharajas*, pp. 139, 142, 144–5.

6
A Reformed Sect—the Satsang

The authority of Vallabhachārya was allowed to descend by physical inheritance and no care was taken to set up a teaching order which could promulgate and develop his teachings. This seems to have been the great weakness of the Pushti Marga, one which the founder of the Satsang was careful to avoid. In addition, as we shall see, his doctrine of *bhakti* was more controlled, and his insistence on separation of the sexes absolute.

My experience of the Satsang is intimately associated with the memory of my friend Swāmidās, whose difficulties over the Bombay apples I mentioned earlier. He was a landowner and an efficient business man who included among his concerns an important oil agency and, in his village, a small foundry for making spare parts. He was a major partner in the small company that owned, amongst other things, the irrigation works at Sundarana where he had built a small bungalow in a garden; this I shared as an office with Kishor the manager on the spot, and as a sleeping space with the boys who maintained the pumps. Swāmidās was a dedicated follower of Swāmi Narāyan whom he worshipped as Lord, *avatār* of Krishna. His wife, his large family and many of his relatives had joined him in the sect and he was, unlike many, an active missionary, ready to discuss with anybody the beauties and virtues of the Satsang. I remember witnessing one of those impossible situations, sometimes described by others, when this *bhagat* was confronted by a rather simple-minded young Jesuit who was visiting me one day. Swāmidās sat down to enjoy a conversation about God with a fellow *bhagat*. His own position was clear enough: Jesus Christ, Mohammed, Buddha, were all manifestations to different peoples at different times of the one Lord, Swāmi Narāyan. The attitude of the priest was simpler still; as Swāmidās drove me home to his village for lunch he came as near to condemning a man as I ever heard him do. It had not, I think, occurred to him that one could condemn someone else's beliefs as not merely erroneous, but as positively false and evil.

I first met Swāmidās entirely by chance. I was making a tour of the villages in the very early days looking for one in which to settle. My criteria were of the vaguest; I suppose I had some relatively manageable size in mind. My guide was a distant relative of Swāmidās who, naturally, took me to see his wealthy kinsman. Swāmidās took charge of me immediately in a very endearing and unpossessive way, introduced me to the group of his regular friends who met at least once a day in his office to drink tea, chose Sundarana for me and drove me out there that day. After I had been settled in Sundarana for about a week Swāmidās turned up one day with an already over-crowded car and announced that they were off to Vadtāl; it was *punam*, the festival of the full moon.

The journey to Vadtāl took us about an hour, we travelled in the heat of the day, arriving at about three o'clock in the afternoon. Almost immediately we went in to have *darshan*.

The temple, built in the nineteenth century, is on much the same scale as a rural parish church in England of the same period. The exterior is not ornate, but the internal stonework is covered in pictures executed in rather harsh colours. According to tradition, Swāmi Narāyan himself participated in its construction. The building is dedicated to Laxminarāyan, which is to say Vishnu in association with

Laxshmi, goddess of good fortune. Stone steps lead up to the main entrance, and on the threshold one is confronted by three alcoves, or shrines, occupying the far wall. In these are set, three by three, various images, their names painted in black on the wall above. In front of these shrines runs a rail which constrains the faithful to pass in file, and the order is from right to left.

The central image and the largest is, as one might expect, that of Laxminarāyan, but it is not the most important. It is the image on the observer's far left as he enters the temple which receives the greatest veneration, the image to which the worshipper comes last. It is believed to be the *svarupa* of Swami Narayan, and he is said to have pronounced an identity between it, his historical fleshly existence and his being in heaven. The shift of importance from the central image to the *svarupa* of the Swami reflects something of the changes which occurred in his own lifetime, as we shall shortly see.

After *darshan* we joined our friends in the temple court-yard and it was interesting to note, from an aside to one of his friends, that Swāmidās had expected me to have some special experience as I had *darshan* of that final image. In reply to the half-heard inquiry I heard him say, 'No, not yet.'

We then visited the buildings which face on to the four sides of the temple courtyard. A large part of these is given over to the ascetic members of the sect and the temple priesthood. Others are crowded with relics of Swāmi Narāyan. Each room is a shrine and there are many life-size representations of Swāmi Narāyan made of painted wood. These were very different from the *svarupa* image in the temple which, like most representations of the deity in Gujarati temples, made no attempt at realism and was the usual large-eyed, highly stylized form.

As Swāmi Narāyan died in 1830 and, in the course of his lifetime, achieved divinity, or something like it, it is not surprising that the number of relics is considerable. Individual items which stand out in the memory are an entire bullock-cart in which he made a journey, an ornamental *gadi*, a large raised seat from which he preached, and a much venerated paper bearing his footprints in red. Apart from these, there were piles of wooden sandals, heaps of rosaries, turbans, coats, *dhoti* and other articles of dress. I said earlier that any holy man who wins the devotion of a family is likely to leave some article of dress, a cooking vessel or a sandal behind him as a memorial. It is not difficult to imagine that, even before Swāmi Narāyan came to be venerated as the Godhead, any article which had been in contact with him should have been carefully preserved.

After this visit to the relics I experienced something very characteristic of this sect. The group of us who had come with Swāmidās, and some others from other villages, all, as far as I could judge, substantial landowners and business-men, forgathered in a room set aside by the temple authorities as a temporary lodgement for one of the preceptors of the sect. This was a very elderly man, a Brahman from Umreth, revered by this particular group as their *guruji*, honoured teacher. He was a married man and a householder, and although he had now given himself up entirely to devotional practices, he had been a substantial landowner and cotton merchant. It was explained to me that the authorities of the sect, fully appreciating the changes taking place in the modern world, had thought it best to appoint such members of the laity whose orthodoxy was unquestioned, but who at the same time were thoroughly conversant with the difficulties and temptations, intellectual doubts and failings of those obliged to live and work in the modern world. He was already in his eighties when I had my *darshan* of him and died shortly afterwards. He was succeeded by one of the group, an energetic and successful lawyer in his mid-fifties.

The *guruji* asked a few questions about myself, my

presence and interests and about Christianity; he also presented me with a scented leaf, *kevaḍo, pandanus odoratissimus*, from the temple. This participated in the sanctity of *prasād*, although it was obviously not for eating. For the rest of the time, about half an hour, we sat in silence while the *guruji* carried on quiet conversation with individuals sitting near him.

After we had sat for about twenty minutes, one of the group got up and abased himself in front of the *guruji* asking leave to withdraw. The *guruji* looked up and said, 'No, sit for ten minutes more.' The man withdrew back to his place. After the ten minutes the *guruji* gave us all leave to depart and only his chief disciple and successor remained with him. I was given to understand afterwards that this imposition of a period of sitting was an important element in the discipline of the sect. Swāmidās told me that it was necessarily arbitrary and the period of sitting might be prolonged for an hour or more. 'Especially when you are young,' he said, 'you're thinking of getting back to your family and your business and it is very necessary to learn that these are secondary things. We have to obey *guruji* without question. If he were to tell me tomorrow to sell my business I'd do it. I wouldn't like it, but I'd do it.'

Apart from these *guru* formally appointed to certain sections of the laity, the local communities of the faithful in the villages tend to throw up their own leaders. In Swāmidās' own village there was such a man with the rather unusual name of Umadbhai, which I take it, derives from the Arabic for noble or illustrious. In my experience it is most uncommon for people in this part of the world not to take their name from a sanskritic name or epithet of God. The only general exception to this, and it is a practice falling into disrepute, is the giving of some derogatory name to a child, such as Dungheap, Punjo, or, another common one, Rooster, Margho, when it is feared that the child might otherwise attract the evil eye or envy.

Umadbhai had married off his children and had sufficient income from his land for his general needs. He devoted himself almost entirely to the study of the sectarian literature and to the worship of the image in the local Swāmi Narāyan temple in the village. After the *guruji*, Swāmidās revered Umadbhai as the authority in his life.

After we had taken leave of *guruji* we piled back into Swāmidās' car and drove back to his village. Whereas on the journey to Vadtāl we had spent our time chatting and joking now the mood was entirely different. Swāmidās and his friends gave themselves over to *japa* which literally means muttering as a man might mutter his prayers. It has taken on a more ritualized significance in sectarian contexts and means the prolonged repetition of a divine name or a supplication. Sometimes the *japa* resembles more one of our own repetitive litanies. On this occasion the group intoned the name Swāmi Narāyan over and over again all the way home.

Although there are many distinctive things about the life and church of Swāmi Narāyan, his beginnings appear to have been very much like those of other great founders of movements in India.[1] He was born in 1781 near Ayodhya. His father was Hariprasād Pande, a Sarvaria Brahman. The boy was named Ghanshyāma, a name of Krishna, and his parents died when he was about nine years old. According to tradition, when he was 'eleven years, three months and one day old' he left home leaving an elder and a younger brother behind him. There is naturally enough very little authentic record of how Ghanshyāma passed the years before he became known in Gujarat. Apart from various miraculous events it seems certain that he passed some of his time among yogis and was formally initiated for a second time as a *sannyāsi*, taking the name Nilkantha Brahmachāri. In Saurashtra 'seven years, one month and eleven days' after he had left his home in Uttar Pradesh he came into contact with the followers of Swāmi Rāmananda and was invited to settle with them. Swāmi Rāmananda was himself away at that time and a letter, written by one of his disciples, describes Nilkantha as follows:

> He is quite young but highly proficient in yoga . . . [He] has yellow hair on his head, a big tulsi bead round his neck, a girdle round his waist, a deerskin, a rosary, a kerchief, a piece of cloth for filtering water and a small manuscript. He does not take any solid food and so all the veins in his body look green in colour; nor does there seem to be any blood in his body, and if a woman's shadow approaches him he vomits. He has too many great and noble qualities to be mentioned in this letter . . .²

The small manuscript referred to may have been a summary of the Bhagavagita, written in his own hand and still preserved at Vadtāl. The tradition is that he learnt of the Gita from his yoga teacher, Gopāla Yogi, whom he had met on his wanderings. His reaction to the presence of women is evidence of the *brahmacharya*, celibacy, which marks his later teaching and organization.

Swāmi Rāmananda, some forty years older than Nilkantha, came from Bihar. As a *sannyāsi* he had been initiated into the teachings of Shankaracharya but had abandoned his *guru* in search of a more personal God. In south India he came under the influence of Rāmanujacharya's teaching, to which I have referred, and this he passed on to Nilkantha. The doctrine of *vishishtadvaitvad*, qualified non-dualism, became the central doctrine in the Satsang of the relation of soul to the divine.

When Swāmi Rāmananda returned to his disciples he found Nilkantha already well established among them and initiated him into his order under the dual name Swāmi Sahājananda and Narāyana. When the historical personality is referred to in the sectarian literature the name Swāmi Sahājananda is most commonly used. Narāyan was the name

which the Swāmi preferred above all others for the divine,
and by the association of himself with that divine he came
to be called Swāmi Narāyan—in which name the name and
the divine are blended.

It seems that even in the lifetime of Swāmi Rāmananda
something more than a mere wandering band of ascetics had
been formed. There were temples in different parts of Gujarat
and an established body of preaching *sādhus*. As Swāmi
Rāmananda came towards the end of his life he persuaded
Sahājananda to succeed him as Achārya. This appointment
over the head of many senior disciples caused some dissen-
sion and there was a schism which appears to have left the
dissenters with the temples, and Sahājananda with the
greater part of the brotherhood. The following years saw a
phenomenal increase in his following. He was clearly an
extremely vigorous preacher and travelled up and down
Gujarat promulgating what seemed to be his quite distinctive ideas. Tradition and the testimony of eye-witnesses
credit him with some extraordinary hypnotic power which
enabled him to put not only individuals but entire congregations into a trance or *samādhi*. This seems to be more than
just another of the miraculous powers with which such
leaders are often accredited. The reports of mass hypnosis
appear to have caused concern to some of the older disciples
who had lived with him under Swāmi Rāmananda, and were
nearly a cause of further schism.[3]

Swāmi Rāmananda must have died round about the year
1800 and Sahājananda therefore took over the leadership
when he was only nineteen years of age, or thereabouts. He
himself died in 1830 by which time his following had
increased to many thousands. The manner in which he built
up and maintained his following, and evolved an organization to meet each increase in size, suggests that he had a
genius for organization.

The first innovatory step that he appears to have taken
was the initiation of his celibate following as *paramhansa*.

K

The word *paramhansa* implies a very high evolution of spirit, and although there may be dispute as to who is a genuine *paramhansa*, there is no doubt that to be one is to have achieved one of the highest orders of asceticism. According to texts the *paramhansa* is *avyaktalinga*, without any external signs, and *avyaktacāra*, having no settled way of life. He does not spend more than one night in the same village, more than five nights in the same town, or more than seven nights in the same field. He discards all the formal external signs which mark the holy man, including the begging bowl. It is said that his stomach should be his begging bowl, and this implies that he should receive no alms other than food, and no more food than his stomach can carry. Some carry this self-abnegation so far as to go entirely naked, some are even described as madmen because they have evolved beyond all social obligation and dependence; they wander without feeling the need to communicate, meditating on the spirit. It is significant that G. S. Ghurye records that an altogether different brand of militant ascetics chose *paramhansa* to lead them in their disputes with Christian missionaries, because only these could be trusted to be free of all prejudice.[4]

Sahājananda used this belief about the *paramhansa*, apparently quite deliberately, to meet the persecution which his followers were suffering. They had incurred the envy and hostility of rival sects and had to suffer physical maltreatment, even death; also they were subject to spiritual danger in that they were sometimes deliberately offered polluted foods. Some of their persecutors went so far as to deprive them of the images, essential objects of their daily worship, to which they had to offer food before they could themselves eat. By elevating them to the rank of *paramhansa* Sahājananda rendered them socially invisible, so to speak; they now bore no external marks which might identify them as a band. Their new status also elevated them above the consideration of purity and impurity, so that while they would make every effort to avoid contaminated food and drink, they could not

suffer the spiritual damage which these things must otherwise inevitably cause. At this period his ascetic followers ate
and drank together without any consideration of their
former caste allegiances.

The literature of the sect represents this move as a
temporary one to meet the difficulties of the times. It is
certain that when both his own position was well established,
and the stabilizing power of British government had begun
to make itself felt, Sahājananda not merely did not initiate
any more *paramhansa*, but strictly forbade his *sādhus* to
abandon caste orthodoxy.

There seems no doubt that the Satsang benefited by the
establishment of British rule in Gujarat. It is believed that
Sahājananda predicted their coming and there is no doubt
that he was regarded by the British officials as a wholesome
and stabilizing element. It is worth quoting at some length
from the journals of Reginald Heber, Bishop of Calcutta,
who, shortly before his death in 1826, made a grand tour
from Calcutta to Bombay.[5] The Bishop arrived in Baroda in
March 1825, and travelled west across the Mahi river into
the Kaira district of Gujarat. On 25 March he camped at
Amod where he recorded an account given him by Mr.
Williamson, the British resident at the court of Baroda,
concerning the general 'state of rebellion' in Saurashtra and
in Kutch. From these regions armed bands made frequent
forays into the fertile areas of central Gujarat which were, at
that time, divided up between the Gaikwad of Baroda and
the British. The Bishop's account continues:

> Some good had been done, Mr. Williamson said, among
> many of these wild people, by the preaching and popu-
> larity of the Hindoo reformer, Swaamee Narain, who had
> been mentioned to me at Baroda.

I break off here to note that the only likely reference in the
Baroda entry is to a 'new sect of Hindoos' about which he
questioned a visiting prince from Saurashtra. He had been

told that this man had attempted to suppress the sect by force of arms and, in reply to the Bishop's question, the prince replied

> in rather a fretful tone that 'there were too many of them,' and in reply to a question, what their religion was?—that 'they had no religion at all, but a hatred of their superiors, and of all lawful authority'.⁶

I resume my quotation from the entry for 25 March.

> His [Swāmi Narāyan] morality was said to be far better than any which could be learned from the Shaster [Anglo-Indian corruption of *shastra*]. He preached a great degree of purity, forbidding his disciples so much as to look on any woman whom they passed. He condemned theft and bloodshed; and those villages and districts which had received him, from being among the worst, were now among the best and most orderly in the provinces. Nor was this all, insomuch as he was said to have destroyed the yoke of caste,—to have preached one God, and, in short, to have made so considerable approaches to the truth, that I could not but hope he might be an appointed instrument to prepare the way for the Gospel.

It was while he was listening to Mr. Williamson's account that he received six visitors who presented him with the normal offering of sweets and announced that the 'Pundit Swaamee Narain sends his salam'; and, being in the neighbourhood, the Swāmi asked permission to call on the Bishop the following day. The Rajput spokesman of the group told him that the old man accompanying them was a Muslim, a servant to one of their number, and, says the Bishop:

> Added that, though of different castes, they were all disciples of Swaamee Narain, and taught to regard each other as brethren.

The Bishop clearly implies here that the Muslim was a member of the Satsang and this may, indeed, have been possible at that time. Even today there are many Muslims in Gujarat whose knowledge of their own faith is shadowy in the extreme and who may well revere local holy men, just as Momad participated in the *bhajan mandali* in Sundarana, without for all that imagining that they are obliged to renounce such Islam as they have. Today actual membership of the sect would involve a more formal commitment.

On 26 March Bishop Heber arrived at Nadiad, a large important town of the Kaira district, mentioned as early as 1638 by Mandelslo as a 'centre for the production of both cotton and indigo'.[7]

About eleven o'clock I had the expected visit from Swaamee Narain, to my interview with whom I had looked forward with an anxiety and eagerness which, if he had known it, would, perhaps, have flattered him. He came in a somewhat different style from all which I had expected, having with him near two hundred horsemen, mostly well armed with matchlocks and swords, and several of them with coats of mail and spears. Besides them he had a large rabble on foot, with bows and arrows;

The Bishop reflects wryly that his own retinue was considerably smaller and laments the fact that two religious teachers should meet 'with the rattling of quivers, the clash of shields, and the tramp of the warhorse'. He does make the point, however, that his own troops 'though less numerous, would have been, doubtless, far more effective, from the superiority of arms and discipline'. He goes on to compare the attitude of his own troops, who guarded him because they were ordered to do so, with the guards of the Swāmi, who were in addition his ardent admirers and disciples. After expressing great hope that one day a Christian minister might be so surrounded in India, he goes on to describe his meeting with Sahājananda:

The holy man . . . was a middle-sized, thin, plain looking person, about my own age, [42] with a mild and diffident expression of countenance, but nothing about him indicative of any extraordinary talent.

He seated the Swāmi on his right hand, and after the usual civilities invited him to meet him at Kaira Town 'where we should have more leisure'. The Bishop's hope was that at Kaira he would be able to present Sahājananda with a copy of the scriptures in Devnagari and further persuade him to go with him to Bombay:

Where I hope that by conciliatory treatment, and the conversation to which I might introduce him with the Church Missionary Society established in that neighbourhood, I might do him more good than I could otherwise hope to do.

Sahājananda declined the invitation saying that he was extremely busy; he had five thousand disciples in the neighbouring villages whom he was now visiting. In the following week some fifty thousand from different parts of Gujarat were due to assemble for the occasion of his nephew's investiture with the *janoi*, sacred thread. If the Bishop were staying longer in the district he, Sahājananda, would be happy to see him once he had got this ceremony out of the way. The Bishop then asked him to divulge some of his teaching and, reports Heber:

He began, indeed, well, professing to believe in one only God, the Maker of all things in Heaven and Earth, who filled all space, upheld and governed all things, and more particularly dwelt in the hearts of those who diligently sought him; but he alarmed me by calling the God whom he worshipped, Krishna, and by saying that he came down to earth in ancient times, had been put to death by wicked men through magic, and that since his time many false revelations had been pretended and many false divinities set up.

The grounds for the Bishop's alarm were that 'notwithstanding the traits of resemblance which [this declaration] bore to the history of our Lord', the name Krishna was associated with 'uncleanness and folly in the popular legends'. To the apparent gratification of the Swāmi and his following, the Bishop then asked whether Brahma, rather than Krishna, was not the God and Father of all. Sahājananda 'smiled and bowed and with the air of a man who is giving instruction to a willing and promising pupil', explained that there were indeed many names for the one God: he continued

> But there is a spirit in whom God is more especially, and who cometh from God, and is with God, and is likewise God, who hath made known to men the will of the God and Father of all, whom we call Krishna and worship as God's image, and believe to be the same as the 'Surya' [sun].

The Bishop, obviously struck by this parallel with the doctrines of the incarnation, a parallel which has lost nothing in his rendering of it, thought that he saw a 'fair opportunity' and agreed 'that God is everywhere, and that there is no other besides him'. This gained him a cry of 'Allah Akbar', Victory to Allah, from one of the Muslims in the room. The Bishop then seems to have alienated this supporter by proceeding to a brief outline of the doctrine of the incarnation in terms of the logos and the sonship of Christ. 'Here one of the Mussulmans left the room; perceiving which and being anxious to keep the remainder a little longer', Heber addressed himself to the elderly Muslim attendant who had first announced the Swāmi's intending visit. He appealed to him on the grounds of Mohammed's own writings concerning Mary and Jesus, resting his case on what I take to be

sura III of the Koran, verse 40, which he also takes as
evidence for the Incarnation. He then returned to the Swāmi,
arguing that the word of God which proceeds from and is
one with God, can in no way be equated with the sun 'since
the sun rises and sets, is sometimes on this side of the world
and sometimes on that' whereas God is everywhere. Swāmi
Narāyan appears to have replied that he had not meant to
say that the sun *was* God, but *like* God in brightness and
glory. Their belief was, he continued, that there had been
many *avatāra* in different times and lands and added,
'something like a hint that another *avatāra* of Krishna, or
the Sun, had taken place in himself'.

A little later the Bishop asked for a description of the
form of worship and had the Lord's Prayer recited in
Hindustani as an example. He was misunderstood as asking
in what form God was worshipped and was consequently
confronted with

> a large picture in glaring colours, of a naked man with
> rays proceeding from his face like the sun, and two women
> fanning him; the man white, the women black.

The Bishop's reaction to this was to give Sahājananda to
understand what both Christianity and Islam taught about
image worship, although, as he says, his 'fluency had begun
to fail'.

Having received some 'paltry little prints of his divinity in
various attitudes' the Bishop turned the conversation to ask
the Swāmi's opinions on the system of caste:

> to which he answered, that he did not regard the subject
> as of much importance, but that he wished not to give
> offence; that people might eat separately or together in
> this world but that above . . . pointing to heaven, those
> distinctions would cease where we should be all 'ek ekhee
> jat' [all of one caste].

The interview concluded with the exchange of gifts and

the promise of mutual prayers. It was plain to the Bishop that Sahājananda's 'advances towards truth had not yet been so great' as he had been told, but that he exercised his great power over 'a wild people' to good purpose. The Bishop concludes this section of his entry as follows:

I thought from all which I saw that it would be to no advantage to ask him to accompany me to Bombay.

I have quoted at length from this account of an historic encounter not only because it is amusing in a sad sort of way but also because it fairly represents the reputation which Sahājananda had with the British. The whole conversation, brief as it is, reveals the breadth and the depth of misunderstanding between these two excellent men. It is the only recorded instance of direct contact between Sahājananda and a Christian missionary, but it is likely enough that, given his relatively good relations with British officials, he may subsequently have come to learn something of Christian doctrines. Some elements of the teaching accredited to him by tradition suggest an element of Christian influence, either on his exegetes or upon the faithful more generally. There is, however, no suggestion that he himself was directly influenced nor that the reforms which he preached were instigated with one eye upon British opinion. His message was formulated and promulgated long before they had established themselves as the paramount power in this part of India.

That the British regarded Sahājananda as a force making for 'law and order' is clear from the account given to Bishop Heber by Mr. Williamson. Towards the end of his life in 1830, the Swāmi visited the Governor of Bombay, Sir John Malcolm, then at Rajkot. According to British accounts the Swāmi was accorded a military escort and was met by the Governor and his aides outside the Political Agent's bungalow; once inside the two discoursed on religious matters. On his departure the Swāmi was presented with 'a pair of

shawls and other piece goods' and gave, in his turn, a copy
of his Precepts, known as the *Shikshāpatri*, to the Governor.[8]
In the iconography of the sect this episode is represented
in a contemporary painting which I cannot unfortunately
reproduce here. It depicts Sahājananda seated on a *gādi*,
elevated on a dais, and surrounded by his disciples. Before
him, at a respectful distance, stands the Governor of Bombay
and his retinue, wearing what appears to be black official
dress which contrasts sharply with their bright pink, bare
feet. Their bright pink faces are bowed over bright pink
joined hands. This view of the matter is supported by the
manual of devotion known as the *Satsangi Jivanam*, where
the Governor is described as running with all his following
barefooted to greet the Swāmi on his arrival at Rajkot, and
prostrating himself to become his disciple.[9]

What did Sahājananda teach? He is not to be regarded
as a great *achārya* in the traditional sense, in that he did not
propound a distinctive philosophy of his own. On the
contrary he maintains throughout his writings that he
adheres to the *vishistadvaita*, qualified monism, of Rāmanujachārya.

As may well be imagined, the refinements of theology do
not enter into the day-to-day beliefs and practices of the
majority of the sect. This adherence to Rāmanujachārya has,
however, two significant aspects which are worth noting.
In the first place, apart from a few minority sects such as
that of his own preceptor, the dominant influence in Gujarat
of his time was that of the descendants of Vallabhachārya,
from whom Sahājananda wished to dissociate himself. In the
second place the *bhakti* doctrine of Rāmanujachārya is
altogether more complicated, and requires far more discipline, than the same doctrine represented by Vallabhachārya's exegetes.

For Rāmanujachārya *bhakti* is a condition which is dependent upon *karmayoga*, the performance of action, rites and

ceremonies without regard for the fruits resulting from them,

ERRATUM

Page 139, fourth line down of David Pocock: *Mind, Body and Wealth: A Study of Belief and Practice in an Indian Village* should read:

bhakti. Bhakti is itself a yoga and involves purification of the

guishes it quite clearly from what he calls *prapatti*, which corresponds much more to what we in the West would recognize as a blind and simple faith. It requires only a sense of total helplessness and dependent reliance upon God. Significantly this *prapatti* is available to all castes whereas *bhaktiyoga*, as defined by Rāmanujachārya, is limited to the twice-born. The reader will recognize in this *prapatti* the *popular* representation of the *bhakti* doctrine as I have described it earlier, and as it is expounded and practised by Vallabhachārya's descendants. Finally, the greater asceticism and control involved in Rāmanujachārya's *bhaktiyoga* may be associated with a third aspect which clearly separates the followers of Sahājananda from those of Vallabhachārya This is the complete absence of references in Rāmanujachārya's writings to Radha, the divine consort of Krishna, and the consequent lack of emphasis both on *shakti* worship and erotic symbolism.

There are two other tenets of Rāmanujachārya which are clearly active in the Satsang today. These are his doctrine of the soul, and his 'fifth way', *achāryabhimanayoga*, dependence on the preceptor.

For Rāmanuja, as for Sahājananda, the soul is an atomic, eternal, attribute of God and dependent on God. This doctrine is offensive to the monism of Shankarachārya in that it gives substantiality and agency to the soul. It conflicts also with Vallabhachārya's teaching in that it leaves no room for *pushti*, grace, by which God inflames devotion in the individual soul. The doctrine seems to have had an important effect on the members of the Satsang (here I report a strong personal impression) in that they seem more committed than others to getting on with the *job* of their salvation, seeing it as a task in which they actively co-operate. To introduce a distinction, found elsewhere in India, which is applied to two schools of thought deriving from Rāmanujachārya's teaching, the members of the Satsang are like baby monkeys who take a fast grip on their mother's abdomen, and thus are conveyed to safety. Such tenacious souls are contrasted with the kittens which, when in danger, sit and wait for their mothers to carry them away by the scruff of their necks without themselves giving active assistance. The distinction is similar to the Western distinction between salvation through works and salvation through grace.

The *achāryabhimanayoga* is a very interesting doctrine in that it gives a special place to the *achārya, guru* or preceptor, in the salvation of his disciples. This doctrine also requires a total dependence, but now the dependence is upon the preceptor; one submits oneself to him in all matters and without question. The preceptor takes upon himself the business of the disciple's salvation and does all the necessary work. The disciple's contribution is simply his faith and obedience. Sir Ramkrishna Bhandarkar, whose authority must carry great weight, says that this doctrine 'seems suspicious. It has a striking resemblance to the Christian doctrine of Christ's suffering.' He goes on:

> If the prevalence of Christianity in and before the time of Ramanuja in the country about Madras is a proved fact, this doctrine as well as some of the finer points in the theory of Prapatti may be traced to the influence of Christianity.[10]

The traditions of the Satsang record that Sahājananda, when he succeeded Swāmi Rāmananda, asked that he should be allowed to take upon himself the sorrows and misfortunes which his followers might suffer as a result of sins committed in previous incarnations. This can be seen to be a development from, and an expansion of, Rāmanuja's original teaching. If comparisons with Christianity are looked for, we may also note at this point the very strong belief in the sect that at the moment of death Sahājananda appears in person to the dying man to comfort him and take him away.[11]

I have treated these doctrines in a rather cursory manner because the average Satsangi is as ignorant of them as the average Christian is of his own theology and philosophy. I should qualify that remark immediately by saying that the average Satsangi probably does in fact read more of his sacred and approved literature than the average Christian, at least in Anglo-Saxon countries. However, it is still true to say that the basic teaching of Sahājananda, as it affects day-to-day life in society, is contained in the *Shikshāpatri*, the Book of Precepts, which Sahājananda ordered should be worshipped as a representative of his very self, *svarupa*.[12]

Here I would like to draw attention to some aspects of this remarkable work. It strikes the Western mind as a puritanical document by its insistence upon the segregation of the sexes in all sacred matters, the avoidance of sexual sins, and of all the possible circumstances in which they might occur. It is also puritanical in an older sense. The Satsangi who obeys the Precepts emerges as a sober, cautious man of the world. He keeps daily accounts, he pays his workers their due, he is not extravagant either in sacred or secular matters, and even in business dealings involving kinsmen he is careful to have a proper contract drawn up which is signed in the presence of impartial witnesses. He is a man of good sense: in times of disaster and difficulty he will devote himself to the preservation of himself and his dependants and let other duties ride for a while. He is by no means a fanatic and recognizes that the Precepts, whether they relate to spiritual or secular matters, must be adapted to the circumstances of time, place, age, means and rank.

What I myself find most striking about the *Shikshāpatri* is its very marked sectarian quality; it lays down very precisely the kind of worship in which a Satsangi may involve himself. Those precepts which positively enjoin certain kinds of behaviour are not so remarkable as those which expressly forbid, or modify, certain others. Almost every work of a similar nature, addressed to a lay following, will prescribe what marks must be worn on the brow, where and in what way the divine is to be worshipped. But these injunctions are usually added to the accumulated body of beliefs and practice, and seldom act in such a way as to modify or preclude some of them. There is, in other words, a tendency in the *Shikshāpatri* towards a kind of exclusivism, an absolutism, which seems to me to mark a radical innovation. This has certainly developed since Sahājananda's time, as I shall shortly describe.

The new tendency is most marked in the way in which the *Shikshāpatri* makes it quite impossible for a Satsangi to be in any way involved in what I have called the impure cult. They are not to eat the *prasād* of Kāli because she is usually offered flesh or liquor. They are not to eat the *prasād* even of Krishna if the offering has, in the first place, been made by a man of inferior caste. When troubled by a ghost the Satsangi will have recourse to the *mantra* laid down by Sahājananda and not to that of an 'inferior' god: both the Sanskrit and Gujarati are quite explicit here, the word is *kshud* which means trifling, petty, worthless. Shiva is to be accepted with Narāyan as one god, but only images which have been sanctified by the *achārya* are to be worshipped, that is offered *puja*. To other images an obeisance is sufficient. If the Satsangi happens upon a Shiva temple, or the temple of some other god, he should make obeisance and go in for *darshan*, but no more.

The Pushti Marga of Vallabachārya is referred to explicitly only once when the fasts, festivals, and modes of worship laid down by Vallabhachārya's son Vitthal are also prescribed for the members of the Satsang. There are, however, several implicit references to the known practices of that sect. The *achārya*, for example, may not initiate a woman; that is left to his wife. The reference in verses 73–4 to 'unrighteous acts performed by great persons in the past' which are not to be imitated, preclude the acceptance of some of Krishna's amorous adventures as examples for emulation. The injunction on ascetics, that they are to have nothing to do with men dressed as women, refers to some of the more dramatic performances in the rituals of the Pushti Marga. In short Sahajananda in his *Shikshāpatri* set an example of worldly good sense for his followers, in that he avoids any direct critical reference to that body of believers from which he was most concerned to dissociate his following, while tacitly achieving his ends.

I have several times referred to Sahājananda's capacity as an organizer. The sect has not been entirely free of schism, nor has it been able to avoid the disputes over property which almost inevitably arise once wealth has been accumulated. However, the fact that it has avoided these evils to a great extent, and continued to grow in numbers and reputation, is due in large part to Sahājananda's foresight.

There is some doubt as to whether Vallabhachārya was himself a *sannyāsi* or not. It is certain, however, that the subsequent teaching of his sect discounts the advantages of asceticism. A by-product of this emphasis, regretted by some present-day members of the sect as much as by sympathizers outside it, is the lack of any group in the Pushti Marga dedicated to scholarship and the ongoing exegesis of Vallabhachārya's doctrine. Vitthal, who may be regarded as the second founder of the sect, seems to have been an imaginative genius in matters of ritual and associated beliefs, but he committed his entire inheritance to his heredity. His sons and their descendants were the sole recipients of spiritual authority from the past, and immense adulation and wealth from the present. In such circumstances it is not surprising that the tradition of learning tended, with some exceptions, to be lost, and that the Maharajas came to be surrounded with a corrupting veneration more appropriate to images.

I have mentioned Sahājananda's use of the *paramhansa* concept to free his *sādhus* from persecution. His first major act of organization also related to the *sādhu* body which, at the time of his death, amounted to something over three thousand. As can be seen in the *Shikshāpatri*, Sahājananda divided his *sādhus* according to their castes and, by thus abandoning the *paramhansa* notion, almost certainly increased their numbers. Some years before he died he also divided them up into sections under *sādguru* to whom they were subject in spiritual and disciplinary matters. Later, to avoid rivalries and unedifying competition, the *sādhus* associated with particular temples were allocated 'parishes' within which to preach.

This allocation of particular *sādhu* to particular areas was a recognition that the following of Sahājananda now included a substantial body of the laity; the realization that he had particular spiritual obligations to this laity marks, I think, the development from a movement to a sect, or even Church. This growth was made certain in the last decade of his life which saw the building of the three most important temples of Ahmedabad, Vadtāl and Gadhada. Since that time many other temples have been built and Satsangis have carried their faith to East Africa and to Fiji, but these three original temples remain the chief centres of pilgrimage.

The accumulation of property raised questions and problems of ownership, and to meet these Sahājananda had recourse to heredity. He adopted the eldest sons of his elder and younger brother and appointed them *achārya* of the North and South. In their hands was vested the property of the Satsang and the rite of formal initiation.[13] The two *achārya* were to be married men and their duties were to devolve on their sons. Although Sahājananda called these two successors *achārya*, philosopher, teacher, their position is rather that of the monarch in the English system as head of the state and church.

The *achārya* are expected to lead exemplary and even edifying lives, but they are not regarded as great sources of insight into the tradition, nor is any great innovation in doctrine expected of them. Typical of their activities is the publication of the Gujarati translation from the Sanskrit of the *Satsingijivanam* which was produced at the order of one of them and of which he is the publisher, located at Vadtāl.[14] All approved editions and translations published by the sect carry on the flyleaf 'By Order of the Acharya Maharaj'. We can say that the material succession of the Satsang has been separated from the spiritual succession in the manner most appropriate to both. The property of the temple is vested in the *achārya*, but it is not his domestic residence, as it would be for the descendants of Vallabhachārya; the development and promulgation of doctrine is in the hands of ascetics and laymen dedicated to the work.

There is little of importance in the history of the *achārya*. There have inevitably been disagreements over the use of funds which have resulted in an increasing limitation of their personal powers. The only scandal which has occurred affected the fourth *achārya* at Vadtāl, who was deposed. Originally the senior *achārya* was based at Ahmedabad and the junior one at Vadtāl, but it appears that the junior line died out after the third generation and the *gādi* of Vadtāl passed into a separate branch of the Ahmedabad family. There have been subsequently several such 'replacements' from line to line in similar circumstances, but it is interesting to note that the hereditary principle is subordinated to the rule that the two *gādi* must be kept separate. Up to the present, no one has sat on either *gādi* who is directly descended from one who has sat on the other.

How does the Satsang appear in the eyes of outsiders, and how does membership of the sect affect beliefs about caste status? I visited Vadtāl several times with Swāmidās and

L

only once without him. This was when I was visiting the nearby village of Jor, a village with which the Patidar of Sundarana had strong marriage relations. My companion was Kishor and, as he had not been to Vadtāl, he suggested that we take it in on our way home. We walked into the temple compound and were making our way up the steps to the main door when one of the attendants shouted out and drew our attention to a large notice that I had not observed before, hanging over the main door. The message was simple: the temple was the private property of the Satsang and only initiated believers were permitted within. Kishor was extremely put out by this incident; on the way home in the train I had to listen to a mixture of mumble and tirade against Swāmi Narāyan and all his works. He represented the Satsang to me as a body of spiritual snobs who thought themselves a cut above everybody else, as a load of hypocrites, as a rich man's club whose sole purpose was to assist its members in business affairs. 'Look at that so-and-so carpenter,' he said, 'there's an uppity bastard for you, if you like. You watch, when they come to the village, he is all over them with his "Jay Swāmi Narāyan". That's how he gets his contracts. *Dhong ane dhandho, saheb, dhong ane dhando*—Sir, it's all hypocrisy and business.'

The carpenter was the only really effective one in the village. He had succeeded in developing a reputation and a trade which went beyond the confines of Sundarana. He was by no means dependent upon such works as even a relatively wealthy man like Kishor could put in his way.

There had been an incident a year or so back when Kishor, after the completion of some work on his house, had invited the carpenter and other workmen to a meal. The carpenter arrived, but when he realized that the food to be served had been cooked by Surajben, a Patidar, he refused to sit down and eat. The Precepts of Swāmi Narāyan do not require that a carpenter should refuse food from a superior caste and insist upon eating food cooked by a Brahman only.

By refusing food from Surajben's kitchen he was making a claim to equality, if not indeed superiority of status. As a man of relative financial independence he could tell Kishor what to do with his food, and the very act of rejection gave him, automatically, some standing in the eyes of other less fortunately placed villagers.

His refusal to eat food cooked by Surajben does not, however, imply that he would refuse to eat food cooked by, shall we say, Swāmidās' wife, nor would this be directly because both he and Swāmidās were members of the same sect. In the first place the carpenter would be concerned with his own status in his own village and, to the extent that he was concerned to better himself, he would wish to assert this status against the Patidar of his own village. In other words it would not occur to him to assert his status absolutely over against all Patidar everywhere. In his eyes, as indeed in all our eyes, Swāmidās stood far beyond any comparison with Kishor.

Among the suburban British the fact that our neighbour has his house front painted may stimulate us to do something about our own flaking and dingy exteriors, but the façade of Buckingham Palace does not stimulate us to paint our guttering. We cannot analyse the carpenter's motives in joining the Satsang: Swāmidās was one of the local gentry whose business he was naturally happy to have. In addition, he represented for many an example of the good life in every sense. Membership of the Satsang allowed the carpenter to participate, in however limited a way, in that same good life in such a way as could only heighten his self-respect. More formally we should note that the carpenter, as an independent individual, could only, so to speak, score points off Kishor in the caste game. However autonomous he might be in spirit and material means he was still a member of the carpenter caste and, as such, inferior to the meanest Patidar in Sundarana. In the Satsang, on the other hand, even though the hierarchy of caste is recognized, membership is by the free adherence of the individual whose caste is, second-arily, then taken into account. In this sense the implication of sect membership accords with the doctrine of *bhakti*, whether that is understood as an emotional dependence upon the divine or the disciplined achievement of self-knowledge.

Kishor had, no doubt, his own legitimate grounds for grievance. The days on which he had to present his account book for Swāmidās' inspection were invariably tiresome. He would bath and shave with particular care, and have his household in an uproar while his fine lawn shirt and best *dhoti* were looked out. On his return he was frequently in an evil temper, in reaction, no doubt, to the deferential submis-siveness which he had had to display during the day. When his senior partners visited Sundarana, Kishor was reduced to the status of a superior servant and was not expected to sit and take tea with them.

It is worth pausing here and considering what else we can learn from the relationship of Swāmidās, Kishor and the carpenter. I said that Kishor would not be expected to sit down and take tea with Swāmidās and his friends when they visited Sundarana in the evening. I must qualify this: if Swāmidās were in an expansive mood and the evening chilly he might well order tea all round. Tea in Gujarat is served nowadays in cups with saucers and when there is a largish company then the cup is the serving vessel and the saucer the drinking vessel. In this way one cup serves two to three saucersful of tea. The cup is formally intended for the person to whom it is first given and he may indeed drink it all. But when there is company, politeness, generosity or thoughts of *najar* may lead him to pour only a saucerful for himself and pass the cup; or he may pour a saucerful for someone else, hand it to him and drink the remainder himself. Certainly if he pours for someone else there is an implication both that he is the superior, and that he is making a gift. If, on the other hand, he passes the cup the suggestion is that he regards the person to whom he passes it as an equal.

If all the company in the courtyard of the Irrigation Works, Kishor and his employees—Patidar, Bareia and Patenwadia— were drinking tea, Swāmidās would pass the cup to Kishor if he were sitting by him, but if the carpenter had joined them he would very likely pour out a saucerful for him. However, tea, especially in the way that it is made in Gujarat, is costly both in itself and for the milk and sugar which is required. Most evenings Swāmidās would call for tea for himself and his friends to the exclusion of Kishor and the others. By so doing he would draw attention to the fact that Kishor was only a junior partner and, to all intents and appearances, an employee.

On one such occasion the carpenter had come down from the village to have a word with Swāmidās. He sat respectfully on the ground a little outside the circle of Swāmidās and his group, who were sitting on concrete benches. Swāmidās asked him if he would take tea and the carpenter, politely joining his palms, excused himself. Swāmidās insisted and simultaneously poured a saucerful which he handed to the carpenter. The carpenter was not in such frequent attendance that this constituted a precedent, but it was clearly a mark of favour such as Kishor did not receive even though, when he did drink tea with Swāmidās, he would, as befitted a caste fellow, receive the cup and not the saucer given to the inferior carpenter.

To sum up: let us imagine that all are drinking tea, the carpenter included. It is quite unthinkable that the carpenter should receive a cup before Kishor, let alone that he should pass it to Kishor or, still worse, pour a saucerful for him. Would Kishor pour a saucerful of tea for the carpenter? This is a delicate question. There is no doubt that as a member of a superior caste Kishor could behave in this way, but we have already seen that the carpenter is sensitive on such matters. My guess is that the carpenter, being the man he was, would politely decline tea from the outset if he saw the risk of such a situation emerging. As for Kishor himself, again I guess, he would not like to run the risk of receiving yet another public rebuff from the carpenter. It is worth noting, incidentally, that the outside observer might not even notice such a rebuff were it offered. The carpenter might very well politely receive the saucer of tea at Kishor's hands and simply put it on the ground in front of him as though he were about to drink it in a little while. He could then appear to forget about it until it was too cold to drink and then with due apologies simply pour it into the earth: Kishor and others would take the point. Questions of personality aside, I conceive it possible that, in such circumstances, Kishor could pass the cup for the carpenter to serve himself and the carpenter could receive it. By doing this Kishor would forfeit nothing since the cup came from not to him, and the carpenter could accept it in so far as he would not appear to be treated as an inferior.

Are Swāmidās and the carpenter friends? People are sometimes led by the descriptions of traditional Indian society to imagine a world of rigid exclusiveness in all matters so strong as to preclude relationships which we would think of as friendly. Obsessed as we may be with the lingering values of class in our own society, the evident facts of inequality of opportunity and of economic conditions, we are still very far from the world of hierarchy. I would go so far as to say that the very rigidity of caste rule defines a fairly precise area in which people can have warm relationships of trust and confidence. When we know with precision and in detail exactly what we must not do, we have the greater freedom to do everything else.

A Patidar landowner sits down in the field to chat with his Untouchable labourer about anything under the sun, and with a degree of intimacy which depends on personal temperament and the length of their relationship. I venture to say that the two men communicate with greater ease and frankness than would an English bank manager and his junior employee, if they happened to run into each other in a pub.[15]

Let me give the extreme example: some Patidar in Sundarana have mistresses among the Untouchables. In some cases, it is said, the husbands connive at the relationships for the sake of the money that it brings in. The Patidar returns to sleep at his own home, and his morning bath washes off the pollution of both copulation and physical contact with an Untouchable. Such relationships are often of long standing but it would not occur to the woman nor to the man that he should or could drink or eat at her hands in her home, or wherever else they might meet.

It follows from this that Swāmidās and the carpenter could be friends. In fact I do not think they were but the Satsang provides a language and an arena within which relationships like friendship, quite compatible with caste, can develop. What is of particular interest in the study of sects generally in modern India is the extent to which the relationships which they encourage correspond to growing political, economic and more general social interests shared by people of different castes—the extent to which these relationships begin to transcend caste relationships, and the extent to which a sect like the Satsang appears to encourage this transcendence.

It is a commonplace of Indian history that the sect which opposes caste regulations becomes, finally, itself a caste. Such has been the fate of the Lingayats of southern India in the past and, more recently, of the Arya Samāj. The precepts of Swāmi Narāyan fully endorse the regulations of caste, and there is nothing in the modern teaching of the sect to suggest that its leaders or influential men in any way encourage neglect of caste prescriptions. From this point of view the Satsang is essentially no different from the other sects of which we have record. If today its members stand apart from their surrounding societies, and at the same time seem to bear witness to certain changes taking place in society, it is as a result of a variety of historical and social factors.

Most generally we can say that the Vaishnavite revival in the fifteenth and sixteenth centuries, coinciding with the establishment of Mogul power, introduced in north and western India a doctrine which ran counter to the older belief underlying the symbiotic relation of pure and impure acted out in traditional rituals.

Even if the followers of Valabhachārya went along with the animal sacrifices which were a part of village life, and even if, on certain occasions, they assisted at blood sacrifices in *mātā* temples, the doctrine of Vallabhachārya and the temple worship laid down by his son were essentially non-violent. Whatever else may have been attributed to the Maharajas, they never tolerated blood sacrifice in their temples. It is very likely, also, that Jainism, which established itself much earlier as the preferred sect of the higher commercial castes, had given added prestige to vegetarian and non-violent worship, even if it did not make many converts among the lower castes of Gujarat.

Swāmi Narāyan's own earliest following was amongst the turbulent lower castes of Saurashtra, and the British administrators, who were soon to follow him, admired the order and peaceableness that he preached. By the petty Rajput princes of Saurashtra, he was, however, regarded as a heretic because he formally denounced in set terms the *shaktipuja* surrounding the worship of Shiva, a cult which the Rajputs themselves, as Shivaites, endorsed.

The rapid decline of the Rajput ascendancy under the British left Swāmi Narāyan with no opponent in the countryside. The higher commercial castes, notably the Bania, were already dedicated to either Jainism or the Way of Grace, and in the villages he had to encounter no united Brahmanic opposition.

It is striking in Gujarat that although, or perhaps because, there are so many Brahman castes we do not find that association of one particular Brahman caste with another non-Brahman caste such as we find in other parts of India, and as may have existed in the past. Wherever we go we find different Brahmans serving one and the same caste even though these same Brahmans may dispute amongst themselves their relative places in the Brahmanic hierarchy. Among the Patidar this indifference goes so far that when a man is marrying his daughter into another family he does not even inquire the name of that family's Brahman; it is a matter of total unconcern to him that the man who performs the wedding ceremony is not of the same Brahman caste as his own family priest. It would, then, have been very difficult, if not totally impossible, for the Brahmans of Gujarat in the nineteenth century to join together and oppose the teachings of Swāmi Narāyan, even if they had wished so to do.

The Satsang has obviously not come into being to meet the needs of a new professional or commercial class in Gujarat, as have various secular associations. Nevertheless it does provide a communion in which the members of the rural-based professional and commercial classes can meet and share a commitment that transcends their separate caste ties. This communion does not contradict the values of caste, and, indeed, to the extent that it raises them to a higher power, membership confers additional prestige. From this point of view we can understand that the carpenter of Sundarana can find in the Satsang an arena within which he can make a social advance, meet with influential men, and enjoy their patronage as much as their edifying conversation.

Although the teachings of Swāmi Narāyan were not directed against caste, the theological exclusiveness which is, I believe, a distinctive feature of his doctrine does, other circumstances favouring, tend to reduce the importance of caste in the eyes of his followers; obedience to caste regulations is contingent upon the authority of the Satsang. Just as a visit to Vadtāl at the full moon has replaced a visit to older sacred centres, so *darshan* of the *guru*, and his blessing are, undoubtedly, of more importance than the Brahman's rituals. Although necessary to a man living in the world, the services of the Brahman have been, as it were, secularized. Swāmidās would very naturally have one of his daughters married by a Brahman who served his family, but for him the real marriage would be the blessing of the couple by his *guru*. Apart from marriage, which for a Patidar is the only ceremony at which a Brahman is essential, Swāmidās would call in his *guru* for all those family occasions and celebrations to which another householder, who could afford it, would normally invite a Brahman. The extent to which the demotion of the Brahman, if I may put it that way, has taken place varies from person to person according to wealth and the degree of devotion: among the villagers the tendency is marked, and for the town dwellers it is complete.

I was not surprised when I returned to Sundarana, after an absence of three years, to find that, whereas during my earlier stay I had heard nothing of *gurus* or sectarian allegiances in the village, now many families from both the Patidar and Bareia castes affirmed an allegiance to a *guru* resident in Dakor. This man, a Vaishnavite ascetic who had settled in that holy town, had, in the customary way, gradually built up a following. This following showed signs of developing the more formal appearances of a sect in that the *guru* gave his disciples *diksha*, and invested them with his *kanthi*. Given what we know of Kishor's views on the sect of Swāmi Narāyan, views which as a voluble and influential man he had no doubt propagated, it may seem obvious that, when the villagers of Sundarana, led by the Patidar, sought sectarian respectability, they should not have turned to the Satsang. The direction of their choice has, I believe, a more general significance.[16]

We pick up again one of the underlying themes in the discussion of *najar*: inequality within equality.

Much the same changes, albeit at slower rate, as have occurred in wealthier villages are making themselves felt in Sundarana. They are largely a product of those changes, for the wealthier villages were not only traditionally the models for respectable and emulable customs, but also the bastions of politico-economic power. The Patidar of Sundarana preserve their prestige in the eyes of their inferiors by enjoying the, admittedly qualified, regard of their superior caste fellows. This they could not earn unless they were ready to abandon, however slowly, the customs which these superiors had themselves abandoned.

Traditionally the political and economical power of the Sundarana Patidar over inferior castes was the shadow of the more effective power of wealthier caste fellows. The ancestors of Swāmidās had an almost absolute power over their dependants, and we must remember that among these dependants are to be numbered the ancestors of Kishor and his kin.

New laws, new land regulations, new economic openings for the lower caste, however limited, inhibit Swāmidās and his kind from the baronial exploitation in which his forebears indulged. The continuing prestige of this aristocracy is considerable but it is still only a shadow of the past. Kishor and the Patidar of Sundarana live in the shadow of that shadow.

They cannot hope to realize in material terms the theoretical equality that they share with their wealthy caste fellows. As the standards of these latter relate less and less to caste customs and to purity, and more to the ideals promulgated by sect, the theoretical union of all Patidar is weakened. Swāmidās, for example, is likely to judge Kishor not so much by the dietary habits of his family or the quality of the marriages which it has contracted as by the exclusive standards of his own sect—Kishor is not a Satsangi, the carpenter is.

How could Kishor and his kin join the Satsang? Membership, so far from being a balm, could only be an irritant. Their material condition would be unchanged and they would be more likely than before to share an invidious equality with the carpenters of this world. They would have exchanged one kind of theoretical equality for another, but one which would deprive them of even the shadows of status.

It is, then, understandable that if sectarian adherence is the respectable mode of behaviour, the Patidar of Sundarana should hive off on their own to an allegiance which they share only, or for the most part, with their traditional inferiors in the village. They can still take pride in this allegiance over against the followers of Swāmi Narāyan, and, at least temporarily, find reassurance of their status. They have found a new inequality within equality, but one in which *they* are now the superiors.

It would be entirely misleading if this formulation were to suggest that reassertion of a relative superiority is all that has occurred. The change has much greater significance. The implication is that the ladder of emulation, which enabled us to see the Patidar caste as a unity, is breaking. The Patidar of Sundarana are now more concerned to establish themselves as a separate section with their associated inferior castes, rather than continue to emulate their caste fellows. Indeed, these latter have moved into an area of activity where Kishor and his kinsmen cannot follow without losing status. It would seem then that the breakdown of the various interdependencies between castes are followed, in this case, by a breakdown of the more subtle interdependencies within a caste.

NOTES

1. For an account of the life and teaching of Swāmi Narāyan, see Bhai Manilal C. Parekh, *Sri Swami Narayana, a gospel of Bahgwat-Dharma or God in Redemptive Action*, Rajkot, 1936.
2. Ibid. p. 211.
3. Ibid. pp. 55–61.
4. Ghurye, op. cit., pp. 122–3.
5. Reginald Heber, *Narrative of a Journey through the Upper Provinces of India, 1824 to 1825*, London, 1828.

6. Ibid., see entry for 23 March 1825.
7. M. S. Commissariat, *Mandelslo's Travels in Western India* (A.D. 1638–9), Calcutta, 1931, p. 19.
8. Bhai Manilal Parekh, op. cit., 1936, p. 299.
9. *Satsangijivanam*, Vol. 2, pp. 355–61, composed by Shatānandmuni, printed and published from the temple of Vadtal on the order of Ānandprasādmahārājashri, Bombay, Samvat 1992, A.D. 1936. This is a compilation of nearly 17,000 verses in five volumes; the longest work composed under the direct supervision of Sahajananda, it lays down in detail the organization and duties of the fellowship. Sir John Malcolm is not mentioned by name in the original.
10. Bhandarkar, op. cit., pp. 80–1.
11. Bhai Manilal C. Parekh, op. cit., 1937, Chap. XIX, places great emphasis upon this belief which began even in the lifetime of Sahajanda. Parekh insists upon the uniqueness of the belief among the sects in India and rejects the apparent similarity with Christianity.
12. For a complete translation see Bhai Manilal Parekh, 1936, Appendix I.
13. The initiation is simple but worth a note. The novice offers water near the feet of the *acharya* and repeats the dedication: 'To Swāminarāyan I give my mind and wealth and the sins of [previous] births'—*man, dhan ane janamnā pāp*. The traditional phrase implying total dedication and one certainly used in the Pushti Marga is *tan-man-dhan*—body, mind and wealth. *Tan* means not only body but also offspring and its omission from the Satsangi formula is significant in the light of the Maharaja Libel Case.
14. See note 33.
15. Choto, for example, inherited from his father a master-servant relationship with an Untouchable family. Although he was in no economic position to maintain them these Untouchables would occasionally come out to his bit of field and help out. I have seen him sit on a day bed out in fields while the old Untouchable woman sat on the ground before him. He would throw her a *bidi* to smoke rather than suffer the contamination transmitted by passing it: despite all this she would advise and berate him about his family affairs and private life, as befitted an old woman who knew more and better than he.
16. The movement has produced a substantial body of literature. H. T. Dave, *Shree Swaminarayan*, Bochasan and Bombay, 1967, gives an account in English of the Swami's life and teaching as received by the movement. I take this opportunity to thank Shri Praful Patel for lending me his copy autographed by the present Guruji.

7

The Contempory Need—*Guruji*

The substitution of the fellowship of sect for that of caste has more far-reaching implications. For all that caste differences and status are preserved within the sect, these are now defined by and confined within a theology which remains, despite all accommodations, egalitarian in spirit. As the wealthy Patidar withdraw more and more from the day-to-day actualities of caste ties, and as these ties progressively weaken in the poorer sections of the caste, this latent potentiality for equality is increasingly realized.

I find support for this proposition in the history of the Satsang. It is, from my point of view, striking that the extension of the sect beyond Gujarat into East Africa, Fiji, and Great Britain, not to mention the cities of India, is not the achievement of the orthodox but of the schismatic movement.

How can we account for this? The original well-ordered sect, with the efficient teaching orders, its literature and evolving theology, seems ideally suited for missionary activity. In part we must attribute what amounts to a lethargy in these matters to a growing preoccupation, accompanied by investment, with the embellishment of the sect. Each village where the sect has substantial representation vies with others in the creation of its own temples. Although missionary activity was not and is not lacking, the Satsangis, more than other sectarians, have been keen to propagate their faith; but the activity was local and directed to the conversion of existing relationships with caste fellows, affines and business associates, rather than to the creation of entirely new ones.

The difference between the orthodox and schismatic movements may initially be characterized by their appeal to two generations, because the younger represents in many ways the styles and problems of the modern city dweller and the emigré.

Well-to-do farmers have worn the *dhoti* all their lives, have visited Baroda, Ahmedabad and Bombay for business purposes, dealt with Japanese, British and American exporting firms and, with all their fluency in the *mechanics* of the Western world, preserved their cultural orthodoxy without taint. Their children have grown up in a different world, a world of cafés, cinemas and discotheques. Their clothes are not the pale imitations of Western modes derived from the memories of a cantonment tailor, but mass-produced, modern fashions imported from the West: they are altogether more familiar than their fathers with the variety and potentialities of modern India.

This generation does not live compassed about with a cloud of witnesses in the village, and needs more than the memory of maternal training to justify to itself the maintenance of a distinctive mode of life. The ethical problems which it faces are, moreover, those of a world with which its parents are conversant but not intimate. The preoccupation of the orthodox with the conversion of their traditional world has, perhaps, led to the neglect of this new generation. A schismatic movement now speaks to the young men and the men of the new professional classes.

What is the significance of this movement and how did it arise? Swāmi Narāyan organized his sect with foresight and efficiency. On one point he departed from traditional practice in that, unlike his own *guru*, Rāmananda, he chose first to split his secular from his spiritual authority, and second to diffuse the latter through the teaching order. According to the orthodox history, and from now onwards I shall have to use this distinction, he did not appoint a particular spiritual inheritor. To this extent his doctrines, organization and rituals were invested with the godhead attributed to him: while the success and stability of the Satsang derives in great part from this fact, it was at the cost of flexibility beyond a certain degree.

The authority and importance of individual guidance is, no doubt, strong. The *guru* is venerated because he is regarded as having proceeded those few steps further towards realization than his disciple. Enlightened and holy he may be, but he is still mortal. He cannot claim revelatory powers superior to those of the historical Sahājananda nor receive worship which might equate him with the divine Swāmi Narāyan. The original movement has slowed down and to a great extent it has crystallized into a Church.

The schismatics derive their history from one of the original *sādgaru* (above, p. 144), known in the literature as Gunatitananda Swāmi, the appointed head of the temple at Junagadh in Saurasthra. He is identified with one who, before his initiation as a *sannyāsi*, was known as Mulji Sharma. This Mulji Sharma is also named in the literature of the orthodox as one of the early disciples of Swāmi Rāmananda. Mulji Sharma was one of the Swāmi's following when Sahājananda, then Nilkanth, first appeared among them. His significance may be seen in the following, taken from a pamphlet published in English from the schismatic temple at Bochasan in the Kaira District.

> Shree Ramanand Swami introduces to Lord Swaminarayan, Moolji [*sic*] Sharma, one of his disciples. Seeing him, Swaminarayan says, 'This Moolji Sharma is the embodiment incarnate of Akshar Brahman—my Eternal Abode. He has the fullest realization of my full-fledged Divine form. With this realized knowledge of my Divine form, he is constantly attached to me. He will spread this knowledge among my disciples and this knowledge alone

of my Divine form, will redeem the souls from the sorrows of life and will transform them to Brahmic state.[1]

The theology here is very complicated. Akshar Brahman is not a place concept like 'heaven', it is a form of Brahman. We need not be concerned with these intricacies, for the essential claim being made here, and it has no parallel in the literature of the orthodox, is that there was a *divine union, a sharing of divinity*, between the man who was to be called Gunatitananda Swāmi and Sahājananda, Swāmi Narāyan. This belief in shared and transmitted divinity has been passed on through four generations of *guru* up to the present time. The document from which I have quoted the story goes on:

> Thus a spiritual legacy was established for the continuous manifestation of the Lord, [continued through such perfectly developed Brahmic personalities] for the redemption of souls.[2]

It is a doctrine, basic to the schismatic teaching, that liberation is achieved by serving the living presence of Brahma which is available in the person of *guruji*, as he is respectfully known.

The difference between the orthodox and the schismatic is comparable with that between the Sunni and Shia muslims. On the one hand we have a learned tradition derived from the teachings of the Prophet Mohammed and his companions, and on the other a movement represented in several sects, each one of which has, at any given time, some kind of inherited divine leadership. The orthodox sect of Swāmi Narāyan leaves room, as we have seen, for what is commonly called '*guru*-worship', but this is controlled by and subordinate to the received traditional doctrine. It was precisely because the third spiritual successor of Gunatitananda Swāmi, Swāmi Yagnapurushdāsji, tried to install an image of Gunantitananda for temple worship that he was obliged

M

to leave the body of the orthodox. It was in his lifetime and afterwards that the schismatics began to establish their own temples.

The schismatics cope with the doubts and difficulties which professional and commercial men are likely to meet in their day-to-day affairs, and in their intercourse with men of very different faiths and ideologies. To the extent that they explicitly and carefully cater for such men they are likely to attract those who have received a largely Western education but wish, at the same time, to preserve a distinctively Indian shape to their lives.

We may imagine a doctor or a lawyer living in Baroda or Ahmedabad, perhaps the third or more generation of city dwellers: what does caste mean to him? He probably calls a barber to his house when he needs a haircut and no doubt the man will be of the Barber caste; but the reason why *he* is called, rather than another, is likely to be that his shop is nearby. Our professional man will send his clothes to a laundry managed, most likely, by a man of the Washerman caste who employs such labour as he can get regardless of caste. Untouchability as represented by particular members of a particular caste will mean little and certainly the scavenging function has been abolished by the water-closet. It is possible that, if his family has been settled in the city for a long time, it may have developed a relationship with a particular Brahman family; but it is equally likely that should our doctor or lawyer wish to marry his daughter he may employ any Brahman whose appearance and manners have commended themselves. In short, the specialization of labour according to pure and impure occupations, the hierarchy of caste and the discrimination that goes therewith, have little basis in modern city life. All that remains is caste endogamy, and even that is crumbling among the younger generation of the educated classes.

Such men can find in the new teaching, as also in other sects, a continuity with the faith of their fathers, and a communion which they can still share with others who more rigidly adhere to the world of caste in the villages.

The orthodox Satsang, synthesizing as it does the values imparted and supported by the village community with the individualistic faith based on *bhakti*, admirably meets the needs of a changing rural society. This synthesis cannot support the modern city dweller and the emigrant, for whom much of the village culture embodied in sectarian practice is meaningless. The schismatic movement, by putting a new emphasis upon *bhakti* and obedience to the *guru*, gives courage to the individual conscience relatively deprived of social support in a situation of continuous change.

Instead of a temple and an image of stone the schismatic movement provides a temple of living flesh in the person of *guruji*, who by virtue of his spiritual succession has authority of revelation and the capacity to preserve flexibility in doctrine and practice.

What we have observed is another variation of the old conflict between priest and prophet. On the one hand we have increasing concern for organization, the insistence on continuity and perpetuation: on the other, an emphasis upon the individual, upon growth, change, and renewal of revelation. In the history of India we witness the final trial of the *sannyāsi*, who has through the centuries fled from the world and been seduced back into it: he suffered modification and corruption by its demands, but preserved and refined, in solitude and in alienation, a language for the loneliness of the permanent emigré, the modern city dweller.

NOTES

1. H. T. Dave, *Brahman Darsham*, Bochasan and Bombay, undated, p. 2.
2. Ibid, p. 6.

APPENDIX 1
Morality and Non-violence

Many anthropological accounts, especially those which concern belief, stretch the students' credulity to breaking point. However intricate the conceptual system of a given society, the belief of the people concerned is all too often represented as a simple, well-articulated faith. To the extent that no room is allowed for scepticism, doubt, and adjustment, the reader must have difficulty in identifying as human these creatures who seem too good to be true.

Let me give an example: we are told that a peasant woman in India should not attend an auspicious ceremony, such as a marriage, while she is menstruating, and she can only purify herself over a period of days. In some areas, and in some castes, she may speed up the purification by pouring water over herself with a sieve. Because the mesh breaks the water into so many streams, these become the equivalent of so many baths; the woman can purify herself instantaneously and so attend the marriage.

There are two typical reactions to this practice found both among sophisticated city dwellers in India and Western scholars. On the one hand it may be regarded as an amusing superstition, and on the other it may be described as a Pharisaism amounting to hypocrisy. Both these reactions impute a kind of simple-mindedness to the peasant in that the first is of the order, 'these people *really* believe etc.', while the second imputes an essential disbelief in that, it is supposed, the peasant is ready to drop any observance when it does not suit his personal convenience. It is these reactions, rather, that are simple-minded because they limit the range of human possibility to total acceptance or total rejection.

I dare to say that no one who accepted either of these alternative views of a peasant woman's behaviour would be content to have his own behaviour so simplified. If I am correct we then confront a problem: why do we allow assumptions about human nature which do not govern our own relationships to creep into our descriptions of others? I approach this as a technical problem for social anthropologists, rather than as the moral problem which it undoubtedly is also.

Let me point towards an ideal alternative with the following:

The religion of the Dodsons consisted in revering whatever was customary and respectable: it was necessary to be baptised, else one could not be buried in the churchyard, and to take the sacrament before death as a security against more dimly understood peril; but it was of equal necessity to have the proper pall-bearers and well cured hams at one's funeral, and to leave an unimpeachable will. . . . A conspicuous quality in the Dodson character was its genuineness: its vices and virtues alike were phases of a proud, honest egoism, which had a hearty dislike to whatever made against its own credit and interest, and would be frankly hard of speech to inconvenient 'kin', but would never forsake or ignore them—would not let them want bread but only require them to eat it with bitter herbs.

Despite the differences of time and culture, this account of an early nineteenth-century, middle-class family, living in a provincial town not yet cut off from its agricultural context, describes perfectly the psychology of many respectable Patidar families in Gujarat today; the chapter from which it is taken is full of echoes. It is a realistic account of a life which the author herself contrasts with a more romantic view.

> It is a sordid life, you say, this of the Tullivers and Dodsons —irradiated by no sublime principles, no romantic visions, no active, self-renouncing faith—moved by none of those wild, uncontrollable pasions which create the dark shadows of misery and crime—without that primitive rough simplicity of want, that hard, submissive, ill-paid toil, that childlike spelling-out of what nature has written, which gives its poetry to peasant life.

Although anthropologists today are not overtly prone to romanticism of quite this order, they have still to develop a language which could save them from a not dissimilar kind of simplification.

I say 'language' because I do not believe that the social anthropologist, as a person, could possibly lack the necessary sensibility: he could scarcely survive in the field if he did so. But what seems to happen, when it comes to writing up one's material, is that the procedures of the disciplines seem to demand a falsification: each general proposition in the formal account is contradicted by a host of memories of individuals who did *not* believe this, or behave like that.

To set out a mass of anecdotes, which by their very specificity would atomize the whole, is no satisfactory solution. Nor do I suggest that the social anthropologist must at least approach the qualities of one of our greatest novelists if he is to pursue his vocation. What I do suggest is that, as increasingly we free ourselves of misconceptions about scientific procedure, we might widen the range of those from whom we hope to learn. Where an analytic intelligence is combined with a sociological sensibility, as pre-eminently in the work of George Eliot, we can perhaps learn to deepen our own analyses without, for all that, pretending to creative art of the same order.

These considerations only voice a frustration and a hope. In this appendix I do not aim at any such analytic advance; rather, for the lack of it, I attempt to correct one major simplification which distorts not only the Westerner's view of rural India, but also the views of Indian citizens.

The simplification is of the complex which embraces vegetarianism, *ahinsa*—non-violence, and the veneration of the cow.

The Patidar subscribe to the values which make up this complex. This proposition means that other castes ascribe to the Patidar behaviour appropriate to these values and treat them, accordingly, as a relatively high caste. Conformably, no Patidar of the countryside would deny that these values are his and that he should observe them. Who, after all, in our own society would disclaim general probity?

Let us consider first the veneration of the cow which is associated with the buffalo and, to a lesser degree, the *nilgai*, a kind of deer which still roams wild in parts of Gujarat. It is a notorious fact that there is a 'cow problem' in modern India. The Patidar who use bullocks for ploughing and draught, and water buffalo for milk, have no 'problems' with either. The caste hierarchy corresponds to local economic gradations; when a wealthy Patidar finds that his bullock or buffalo is ceasing to be economic, he sells it to a poorer caste fellow, or to a man of lower caste. By this process the beast descends the hierarchy from owner to owner. The speed of its descent is determined by the rate of its physical deterioration. Finally it finds itself among those who are not lacking in scruples but who are not, for all that, scrupulous: 'Thou shalt not kill; but need'st not strive officiously to keep alive' sums up the morality which now determines the animal's fate. Whether it dies by natural means or is assisted by medicine, its carcass finishes up with the Untouchable cobbler who will make sandals or shoes from its skin which may well be worn in the family of the original owner.

In a small community these stages in the life of a beast

are likely to be well known. I have reported the whole process as it was given to me by an informant. However, the farmer who first sets the animal off on its downward path does not feel guilty of 'cow slaughter'. An Englishman who enjoys cheap poultry and eggs neither accepts responsibility for battery farming nor eschews his disapproval of it.

Nilgai are not as numerous as they were, but even a small herd of half a dozen can do a great deal of damage to a standing crop. Monkeys are an even greater menace, for they pull up the growing tobacco plants for sport, and destroy the year's crop in a night. Two such predators, the one cousin to the cow and the other descendant of Hanumān, the monkey god, still constitute a formidable problem for a peasantry dedicated to the proposition that even insect life is sacred.

The *nilgai* is a rare visitor today when it can find little wild protective cover. When a herd is sighted, or known to be in the vicinity, messages are sent to Bhil or Vaghari huntsmen who, with gunshot or poison, eliminate the menace.

Monkeys are a chronic nuisance infesting the trees of every village. The only safeguard is to employ a youth as watchman; with a sling and clods of earth he can chase off a troop before it settles. Such is the theory which, if put into practice, would be a great waste of time and effort. In fact certain young men, Choto among them, develop particular skill with the sling and, as he put it to me, one can never be sure that there is not a stone concealed in a clod of earth. There is some point in killing at least one of the monkeys for these creatures do seem to be reluctant to return to a field where one of their number has been killed.

What can we make of this situation? Choto is poor and looked down upon, not only on that account but also because of the various misdoings which he is the first to proclaim. He has little to hope for and chooses the devil's reputation as his particular expression of despair. No landowner would employ him to murder monkeys: all are impressed with his abilities as a watchman. Stones are not so common in that alluvial soil as to make the sling a too obviously lethal weapon.

One final example concerns a snake. In an early discussion with Kishor I had specifically pressed him with the hypothetical example of a snake falling on to a bed on which his youngest son, at that time Vinod, was lying. I received the reply that I deserved: under no circumstances would one kill a snake, it was *pāp*, a sin, and one must have faith, *vishvās*.

Some months later a situation similar to my hypothetical one occurred in the porch of Kishor's house. One of the boys reported a snake in the rafters. Hāthi, the sole possessor of a shotgun in the village, was called and the snake was summarily blasted out of its nook. Later, Kishor gave a coconut to Bhattiji.

Once again, it would be absurd to speak of hypocrisy. For Kishor the taking of life was a sin he would, in favouring circumstances, avoid: it is the occupation of saints to strive harder. The killing of the snake was a sin, and the offering to Bhattiji an atonement. Kishor would wait to see whether it was sufficient: if within a few months he, or some member of his family, were bitten by a scorpion, or even suffered some less directly related misfortune, it would be evidence that a heavier compensation was being demanded.

To the town-dweller the avoidance of violence is a simple matter. Monkeys are certainly a nuisance, but one against which precautions can be taken. At worst they may ruin a garden, but they cannot destroy a livelihood. In the early monsoon a snake may take refuge in the house, but this is a rare occurrence. In short the observation of *ahinsa* presents few problems in the towns or cities and it is questionable, therefore, whether its dictates can properly be said to belong in the field of morality at all. Are our observances virtuous, or merely conventional, when there is nothing that induces us to alternative courses?

Attitudes towards meat eating are interestingly different. Vegetarianism is derived from Vaishnavite teachings, and in part it is imposed by agricultural life. For the old Rajput landlords meat, but never beef, was permitted; in effect such meat as they ate would have been the product of the chase. Even for those lower castes which were not touched by Vaishnavism, before the advent of Swāmi Narāyan, meat would have been a rare delicacy. The land was increasingly and intensively cultivated to produce the staple crops of millet, and to a certain extent wheat; little was left wild for game. For similar reasons fresh vegetables are still a delicacy for the majority today. No land is afforded for them in the village, and they form no part of the diet of lower castes.

Conceivably because meat was, and still is, the permitted food of Rajputs, a warrior and regal caste, the attitude towards it of even strict vegetarians is equivocal. Readers of Gandhi's autobiography will recall his youthful belief, shared by his contemporaries, that the British owed their strength and political dominance to meat eating. The belief survives in Sundarana.

I bought a bottle of a well-known general tonic for Vinod which appeared to do him good, so much so that Surajben asked me to get another bottle next time I was in town. For all that, I heard from Momad that she was convinced that the efficacy of the tonic was to be attributed to some essence of meat in its content. I assured her, truthfully, that it contained no meat, but she responded with a polite smile, indicating that she was no fool and did not need my reassuring lies. Deeper than the historical example of the Rajputs is, then, this ambivalence hidden in the expression of caste values. The pure is vegetarian, non-violent and superior, the impure non-vegetarian, violent and inferior. Purity finds its ultimate expression in *brahmachārya*, chastity; impurity is associated with genital sexuality. This accords with the belief that the semen, if stored in the body, can be converted into intellectual and spiritual power. It accords also with the villagers' opinion that Untouchable women, although in fact racially indistinguishable, are both more attractive and sexually vigorous than women of higher castes.

The ultimate physical sources of impurity are the activities and excretions common to humanity: birth, menstruation, death, copulation and defecation, blood, sweat and the growth of nails and hair. Village beliefs and morality support a hierarchy which leads away from impure nature while simultaneously accommodating it in a variety of ways. Sin and impurity result from the exigencies of life, they happen to men as inevitably as monkeys attack a tobacco field. The day-to-day morality of the villagers, their pragmatic adaptation of belief to the exigencies of life is in harmony with the symbiotic relation of the pure and the impure. Beliefs about impurity and about violence are not introjected to become matters of choice for an inevitably 'guilty' conscience.

APPENDIX 2
Selections from the *Shikshāpatri* of Swāmi Narāyan

The original book of precepts was written by Swāmi Narāyan in 1830. It is composed of two hundred and twelve tightly packed Sanskrit couplets. It would be very difficult indeed to make a representative selection from so dense a work. What I hope to do here is to give something of the flavour of the thing.

v. 7. Let us all bear in mind the contents of this Shikshapatri with a fixed state of mind as they are productive of good to all living beings.

vv. 11–12. No follower of mine shall ever knowingly kill any creature of any sort . . . my disciples shall never kill any animal . . . for the purpose of offering a sacrifice to the gods . . . for it is declared that *ahinsa* is the highest of all religious duties.

v. 14. Let none ever commit suicide whether through rage, or in any place of pilgrimage . . .

v. 15. Flesh shall never be taken, even though it be the remains of a sacrifice, nor alcohol ever be drunk, not even that which has been offered to the gods.

v. 18. No followers of mine, men or women, shall ever commit adultery, they shall shun gambling and other such vices . . .

v. 19. Nor shall anyone eat or drink from a person of a lower caste, except in Jaganathpuri, even though such things may be the remnants of offerings to Shri Krishna.

v. 23. If any of my followers pass by a temple of Shiva, or other god, he shall bow down respectfully, enter and pay his respects to the image.

v. 24. None shall give up the performances of the duties imposed upon his class or religious order, nor shall he adopt the duties of others . . .

v. 26. You shall not tell such truth as is productive of mischief to yourself or to others . . .

v. 32. Never allow bodily excretions or evacuations or saliva to fall in places protected by the scriptures or public custom from such nuisance.

v. 34. Males shall not listen to discourses on religious matters from the mouths of women . . .

v. 36. Never do any act rashly, neither be slow in religious duties. Impart to others the knowledge you receive, and associate with men of holy living.

v. 39. The worship of Krishna must not be performed without attending to one's secular duties, nor should one give up the worship of Krishna for fear of the calumny of the ignorant.

v. 40. Whether on holy days or ordinary days, men and women in the temples shall avoid touching each other.

v. 48. My followers shall not have resort lightly to the law enjoined for circumstances of extreme distress.

v. 62. Only those images which have been given by the Acharya, or consecrated by him shall be worshipped and given divine service. To other images it is sufficient to make an obeisance.

v. 67. Let everyone always provide his servants with food and clothing in proportion both to their merit and his own means.

v. 68. In conversation every person should be addressed conformably to his position and suitably as to the time and place . . .

vv. 81–82. The fasts and festivals appointed by that king

among Vaishnavas, Shri Vithalanathji, son of Shri Vallabhacharya, shall be observed as he ordained, as shall be the
service prescribed by him for the Lord Krishna.

v. 105. The individual soul dwells in the heart, subtle as
an atom. It is Consciousness and Knowledge. It pervades
the entire body, and is invulnerable, and indivisible.

v. 106. The world of *maya* is the *shakti* of God: it is
known by three qualities—it is darkness, it produces in
the soul ideas of the body and bodily matters, it gives
birth to notions such as I and mine.

v. 107. That which abides in the heart and pervades
the life, ever watchful and independent, which gives the
fruit of actions, that is the Lord.

v. 115. Krishna, his incarnations and the images of those
incarnations are suitable for meditation. Living men, other
gods, and even those who are knowers of Brahman must
not be meditated upon.

vv. 135–136. My male followers who are householders
shall not touch widows other than close relations, nor shall
they remain alone in a private place with a young mother,
sister or daughter except in time of distress.

v. 147. My followers shall give a tithe of grain or money
acquired by their exertions to Krishna, to the poor they
should give a twentieth part.

v. 152. My followers shall pay the wages agreed to
workmen and not keep secret the payment of debts, nor
shall they keep secret transactions at the time of marriage.

v. 154. When they are oppressed by governments my
followers shall leave even their own native country to
emigrate to another and live there in peace.

v. 208. My followers shall read this Shikshapatri daily,
or hear others read it.

v. 209. Even if it is not possible to read it, it should be
worshipped each day and honoured with the highest
reverence as my word and my representative.

v. 212. And may he who destroys the afflictions of the faithful, and preserves the devout observers of *dharma*, who gives happiness to his devotees, may that Lord Krishna grant us all his blessings.

Glossary

In order to avoid distracting the reader I have avoided using diacritical marks in the text except where their pronunciation without such guidance would sound absurd. In this glossary I have given a more careful transliteration for the benefit of anyone who may wish to follow up any particular subject. I have not distinguished the long and the short *i* and *u*: these are often interchangeable in Gujarati.

Some readers may be puzzled by my rendering of *a* in Gujarati words occurring in the text and in the glossary. This results from my concern in the text for a reasonable pronunciation. The name of God, *Nārāyan*, is pronounced with a heavier emphasis on the second *a*; this is reflected in my rendering in the text. The Gujarati short *a* also receives different emphases; although, for example, *kuḷadevi* is the correct transliteration, the *a* tends to be lost in spoken Gujarati. The same vowel, however, in the word *mahādev*, tends to receive a spoken emphasis almost equivalent to the long *ā* which follows it. In general, where *a* occurs without a stress it should be pronounced as the initial vowel in 'again'.

āchārya—a revered preceptor in spiritual matters. Sometimes the word is limited strictly to philosophers who have expounded their own doctrine. The term is not interchangeable with *guru* and connotes much higher authority and prestige.

āchāryābhimānayoga—total dependence upon the *āchārya* not only for instruction but also upon his merits.

advaita—lit. non-duality; *advaitavād*, the doctrine that the individual and the supreme souls are one.

akṣar—letter of the alphabet, written or spoken; destiny; Brahma; the permanent, indestructible abode of Brahma.

ārati—the act of offering incense to an image, particularly the evening offering.

Ārya Samāj—founded by Dayananda Sarasvati, born in Gujarat, 1824, died, of poison it is said, at Ajmere, 1883. His teaching based on the inspired truth of the Vedas had no room for caste. Dayananda was basically a reformist in the sense that much Western theological and social thought was given Vedic sanction in his doctrine. A significant and little known fact is that the first English biography of Dayananda was instigated by Sidney Webb who wrote a preface for it (see Lajput Rai, *The Arya Samaj*, London, 1915).

ātma—the soul or, as first part of a compound, the self—e.g. *ātmaghāt*, suicide.

avatār: an incarnation of the divine; see note 4, p. 80.

avyaktachāra : without settled progress and hence way of life.

avyakalinga—without external signs. The component *linga* here means simply 'sign'; see *linga*, the male symbol.

bagbhagat—a hypocrite, one whose piety is suspect.

bakarākṣas—*baka* was a bird (crane?)-shaped spirit of vanity and cunning destroyed by Krishna. A *rākṣas* is a malevolent demon. The composite term means the ghost of a Brahman which is thought to be particularly powerful.

Bāṇiā, var. *Vāṇia*—the traditional trading, commercial caste of Gujarat.

Bāreia—a low caste claiming Rājput affiliations; in the area of this study the Bāreia are landless and work for the Patidar.

bhagat—a pious man.

N

bhagavān : the commonest name, in this area, for divinity whether specified or not. Very commonly used in profane expletive as 'God' or 'Lord' are used in English.

bhāi—lit. brother; as a suffix to a proper name it connotes respect, and in common usage it is the equivalent of the English 'Mr.'.

bhajan—lit. an act of adoration, a hymn.

bhakta—a devotee.

bhakti—devotion, worship.

bhaṅgi—the scavenging caste whose duties involve the clearing of night-soil and the removal of dead carcasses; the lowest of the untouchable castes.

Bhāṭia—a trading caste located for the most part in Kutch. They were probably the first to establish a trading connexion with the Persian Gulf and with East Africa, from which they derived considerable profit.

bhut—ghost, also demon, *bhutaḍi* (dim.), a female ghost.

bhuvo—the particular devotee of a *mātā* who is possessed by her.

brahmachāri—one who is observing the rules of the first stage of life, *brahmchārya*, a period of study and celibacy. In the writings of Gandhi the latter term becomes synonymous with sexual abstinence.

chuḍel—a female ghost, usually that of a barren woman.

darshan—a seeing; of a god, a holy man or any great personage.

deri—(also *daheri*), a small domed shrine or temple.

dhan—see *tan*.

dharamshāḷā—a lodging for pilgrims or travellers, erected as an act of piety.

dikṣa—precept, initiation, the secret saying given at initiation.

gādi—a dais or throne. From such, preachers might address their congregation and hence the term is extended to refer to the town or city where a religious leader has his seat.

Gosaiṅ—the term is used sometimes for a caste of inferior

pujāri who serve the temples of Shiva; sometimes the term is reserved to a Shivaite ascetic.

gvāla—one of the daily rituals in the Vaishnavite temples. Krishna is thought of as tending his cattle.

haveli (from the Arabic)—a large house or mansion. The term used for their main temple by the Pushti Marga.

hinsa—lit. killing and hence violence. Gandhi developed the moral connotations of this term and extended its negative, *ahinsa*—not killing, to cover a wide range of charitable virtues.

homa—a fire sacrifice.

jajmān—lit. he for whom the sacrifice is performed, the patron of the Brahman; by extension any patron.

janoi—the sacred thread, the outward sign of the twice-born. Normally invested about the time of puberty for males only.

japa—muttering, a prayer made by repetition of a sacred verse or name.

japjapavun—to pass one's time in idleness.

kachcha—food cooked in water or oil which may not be received from a lower caste from whom *pakka* (q.v.) foods might be accepted. The term is extended to mud, as opposed to brick houses, country lanes, and almost anything made of an inferior material where a superior version also exists.

kanku—red turmeric, or saffron used to make auspicious markings and hence, especially, the mark on the brow.

kanthi—a necklace, from *kanth*, throat; especially a necklace of *tulasi* beads worn by a Vaishnavite sectarian.

karma—literally, action. The law of *karma* is normally associated with the belief in re-birth: one's status or the events which occur in this life are the product of good or bad actions in an earlier life.

kul—lineage.

kuladevi—the goddess of a descent group.

kulin—a man who has a lineage, an aristocrat.

ling—phallic representation of Shiva in stone; see *yoni.*

mahādev—lit. great god, a title of Shiva, so commonly used as to amount to an alternative name. Cf. Hari (= Lord) Kṛiṣṇa.

mahārāja—lit. great king, a common form of respectful address to Brahmans; the title of the descendants of Vallabhachārya.

mahātmā—lit. great soul, an exalted and illustrious person.

man—see *tan.*

mangala—the first of the daily rites in a Vaishnavite temple.

mantra—a sacred formula, often a divine name, or verse from a sacred text.

mārga—a road or way; a way of life, a sectarian persuasion.

mātā—with a name suffix, one of the many female goddesses of the village. Used alone the term can connote the one, undivided divinity conceived of as feminine (see *kuladevi*).

māya—the created world; illusion.

mel—filth, faeces; adj. *meluṅ*, filthy, filthy minded, devious, hence *melo mānas*, an evil man, scorcerer.

melo—from *melāvavuṅ*, to mix or mingle. A concourse of people, a fair usually at some sacred centre.

mokṣa—liberation from rebirth—variously described by different schools as a state, or condition of bliss, or of non-being.

murti—image, statue, embodiment; see *svārupa.*

najar—a glimpse or view which, when accompanied by envy, we translate as the evil-eye. Hence *najariuṅ*—a black spot on the face, or a charm to avert the evil eye. The word *najar* appears to be derived from Arabic.

Nārāyan—a name of Vishnu.

pakka—ripe, well cooked, or made, durable. The term is used of macadamized roads and brick houses as opposed to *kachcha*, q.v. It is also used of pure foods cooked with the products of the cow, milk or *ghi*, as opposed to those cooked in water or oil.

paramahaṅsa—the highest order of asceticism; one who has subdued all his senses and achieved complete detachment.

Paṭanwāḍia—a low caste similar to the Bāreia, q.v.

Pāṭidār—agriculturists, the dominant caste of central Gujarat.

prapatti—helpless reliance upon God.

prasād—lit. favour, grace; food distributed after it has been offered to god.

pujāri—the one who offers worship, *pujā*; the officiant in a temple.

punam—the day of the full moon, the last day of the bright half of the month. A bogus folk-etymology derives it from *puṇya*—spiritual merit.

puṣṭi—nourishment, strengthening, divine graces, hence *puṣṭimārga*—the way of grace.

rājabhog—lit. a king's enjoyment, feast; the main rite in a Vaishnavite temple.

Rajput—a warrior, kingly caste, formerly dominant in central Gujarat.

Rāval—a very low but not untouchable caste; traditional occupation, playing drums; associated with spirit possession.

sādhu—a holy ascetic, or any good man of holy and virtuous life. Sometimes, but wrongly, used interchangeably with *saṅnyāsi*, q.v.

sandhya—an evening ritual in a Vaishnavite temple; Krishna is conceived to be returning from the pasture.

saṅnyās—renunciation, the fourth stage of life; *saṅnyāsi*, one who has been initiated into the life of renunciation.

sati—a chaste and virtuous wife and, by extension one who burns herself on her husband's funeral pyre.

satsaṅg—*sat*, true and virtuous + *saṅg*, society or fellowship. The name of the sect founded by Swāmi Nārāyan.

satsaṅgi—a member of the *satsang*.

sātvik—pure, true; used of the qualities of the ideal Brahman, and also of pure vegetable offerings in sacrifice etc.

seva—service, divine service.

shakti—power, activity, the divine female expression of this.

shaktipuja—the worship of the divine *shakti*.

shayana—the final ritual in a Vaishnavite temple when Krishna is put to bed.

Shiva—throughout India one of the most powerful male expressions of the divine.

shivnirmālya—flowers offered to Shiva, a term used for any common, worthless thing.

sringāra—the second of the daily rituals in a Vaishnavite temple, when the image is dressed for the day.

sudhāravuṅ—to improve, reform.

suraṇ—a bulbous root vegetable (*Amorphophallus campanulatus*): commonly eaten on fast-days.

svarupa—own figure or form; natural or real figure, to be distinguished in iconology from *murti*, q.v.

swāmi—lit. lord or proprietor, master. It has come in modern times to become almost exclusively a religious title.

tan—body. The Vaishnavite traditionally dedicated himself, 'tan, man ane dhan', body, mind and wealth, to the Maharajas. See note 13, p. 157.

trishul—a trident, one of the weapons of Shiva; often carried by Shivaite ascetics.

upvās—usually translated as fast, it is in fact severe abstinence from a wide range of foods.

uṭhthāpaṇa—the afternoon ritual in a Vaishnavite temple; the god is conceived of as arising from his siesta.

Vāghari—low-caste hunters and fowlers; a byword for dirtiness.

vāhan—a vehicle, the animal upon which a god or spirit is believed to ride.

vishiṣṭādvaitavād—the qualified monism of Rāmanuja, adhered to and preached by Swāmi Narāyan.

Viṣṇu—together with Shiva, one of the most powerful male expressions of the divine.

yoni—the vulva; the vulvic stone circle in which the *liṅga* is set.

zan—demon, evil spirit.

Index